HOME Improvement

Eight Tools for Effective Parenting

HOME
Improvement

Eight Tools for Effective Parenting

Dr. Scott Turansky
Joanne Miller, RN, BSN

 LIFE JOURNEY®
Bringing Home the Message for Life

COOK COMMUNICATIONS MINISTRIES
Colorado Springs, Colorado • Paris, Ontario
KINGSWAY COMMUNICATIONS LTD
Eastbourne, England

Life Journey® is an imprint of
Cook Communications Ministries, Colorado Springs, CO 80918
Cook Communications, Paris, Ontario
Kingsway Communications, Eastbourne, England

HOME IMPROVEMENT
© 2005 by Effective Parenting, Inc.

First Printing, 2005
Printed in the United States of America
1 2 3 4 5 6 7 8 9 10 Printing/Year 09 08 07 06 05

Library of Congress Cataloging-in-Publication Data

Turansky, Scott, 1957-
    Home imporovement : eight tools for effective parenting / Scott Turansky and Joanne Miller.
        p. cm.
    ISBN 0-7814-4151-X (pbk.)
    1. Child rearing--Religious aspects--Christianity. I. Miller, Joanne, 1960- II. Title.
BV4529.T88 2005
649'.1--dc22
                                    2004024895

The names of people who have come to Effective Parenting for counseling have been changed. Some illustrations combine individual stories in order to protect confidentiality. Stories of the authors' children have been used by permission.

Effective Parenting is a nonprofit corporation committed to the communication of sound, biblical parenting principles through teaching; counseling; and publishing written, audio, and video materials.

An audio series, "Eight Secrets to Highly Effective Parenting," is also available. To obtain a complete resource list or have Dr. Scott Turansky and Joanne Miller present their material live, you may contact
        Effective Parenting
        76 Hopatcong Dr.
        Lawrenceville, NJ 08648-4136
        800-771-8334

www.EffectiveParenting.org
parent@effectiveparenting.org

This book is dedicated, first and above all, to the glory of God. And it is our prayer that many will find the greatest gift of all—life in Jesus Christ.

With Special Thanks

To my wife, Carrie, for her faithfulness to God and to me, and to our delightful children, Joshua, Melissa, Benjamin, Elizabeth, and Megan, who have helped us test these tools.

Scott Turansky

To my husband, Ed, for his unfailing support and encouragement that have been an invaluable contribution to this project, and to our wonderful boys, David and Timothy, whose energy and enthusiasm have inspired me to continue on.

Joanne Miller

Contents

Introduction

O kay, it's your turn," my father said as he handed me (Scott) the keys to the car for the first time. With feelings of excitement coupled with fear, I slid into the driver's seat. I had spent many hours studying how to drive, memorizing speed limits, road signs, emergency procedures, hand signals, and a myriad of other helpful information. I had observed others handle themselves in the driver's seat, watched movies about driving, and listened to lectures about the habits of good drivers. Now it was my turn. I remember putting my hands on the steering wheel and wondering, *What do I do now?* That day, I realized there's a big difference between learning about driving and driving.

Parenting is a lot like that. It's one thing to read books on parenting and find yourself nodding in agreement. Somehow, though, you end up wondering what to do when your four-year-old son has a tantrum in the grocery store or refuses to eat his dinner, when your winsome daughter can't seem to keep her shoes on her feet for more than a few minutes at a time, or when your teenager disrespectfully responds to you. You wonder if all that reading and studying about parenting did any good. *What do I do now?* you ask yourself.

Raising children is one of the most challenging responsibilities a person can have, and all parents find themselves frustrated from time to time. Sometimes they're confused because they just don't know what to do. They feel like the mother who saw her three-year-old son put a nickel into his mouth and swallow it. She immediately picked him up, turned him upside down, and hit him on the back. He then coughed up two dimes. Frantic, she called to her husband outside, "Your son just swallowed a nickel and coughed up two dimes! What should I do?"

The father yelled back, "Keep feeding him nickels!"

Don't you wish all solutions could be that easy?

Too often, parents want instant answers for problems that took weeks or months to develop. Life is demanding; pressures squeeze from every side. But good parenting isn't something we can just do during commercial breaks or while driving children to school. Worthwhile solutions require work before a challenging situation improves. Parenting is indeed a lifetime investment.

This book explains and illustrates eight tools that make parenting easier and more effective in our hectic world. Learning and applying these tools will improve your parenting, but they are not a magic formula. They will require work on your part.

In this book, you will meet Craig and Marlene, typical parents who struggle to respond to the day-to-day challenges of raising children. They've been married for nine years and have two children, eight-year-old Jennifer and four-year-old Danny. You'll identify with Craig and Marlene as you see them wanting to guide their children toward maturity—but some days they are just trying to survive. Their questions and feelings may seem familiar to you. Neither Craig nor Marlene had any formal instruction in child rearing, but they've picked up ideas along the way—some helpful and others not so helpful.

This book is divided into eight chapters, each one independent of the others. Feel free to read and reread those chapters that best meet your needs now.

The tools in these chapters have worked for many parents, and they'll work for you. So find a comfortable chair, and journey with Craig and Marlene on their parenting adventure. Who knows? You, too, may learn some things that will change your life.

Chapter 1

Encouraging Obedience Without Yelling

Danny! Stop poking your sister." Marlene glared into her rearview mirror and tightened her grip on the steering wheel.

"She started it." Danny, age four, turned and stuck out his tongue at Jennifer, his eight-year-old sister.

"I did not!" Jennifer scowled. "He always says it's my fault."

Marlene took a deep breath. Why had she thought that taking the kids grocery shopping was a good idea? All the bickering and tantrums on this ride were enough to drive her crazy. By the time she pulled into the driveway, she'd had it.

Releasing her seat belt, she stated, "Each of you grab a bag."

"But Mom," Jennifer whined, "I have to go to the bathroom."

Danny jumped out of the car. "There's Zack with his new bike!"

"Come on, kids! Bring in some groceries. You can take a minute to help." But Danny ran off to Zack's house, and Jennifer headed for the bathroom.

Marlene slammed the car door. "Danny, come back here!" He continued racing down the sidewalk. *They make me so mad. They never listen! It's always the same. They ignore and disobey, and I get mad. Then they're off having a great time, and I'm stuck feeling upset.*

She trudged up the front steps carrying two bags of groceries. *They just ignore me. Life sure would be easier if these kids*

*would learn to think of someone other than themselves. I've
got to do something different.*

The next morning, Marlene walked into the living room.
"Danny, it's time for school. Put those things away and get your
coat." Danny hung over the side of the couch with an action figure in each hand, pretending he hadn't heard her.

*Here we go again. Every morning's like this. I've got to
drop Danny off and be at the office by nine, but getting out of
this house seems to require the skills of a salesman, a drill
sergeant, and a porter all at the same time.*

"Come on, Danny! Put away those toys and get your backpack." She stared at his stocking feet. "Where are your
shoes?"

Danny looked at his feet as if surprised that his shoes were
missing. "I don't know."

"I've told you three times to get your shoes on. Just stand by
the door. Don't move.... I'll go find them." Marlene dashed
down the hall and looked in his bedroom. Then she glanced into
the bathroom. *Yes! There's one. The other can't be far away.
Ah, there it is. In the bathtub? Why can't he just put them on
the first time I tell him?*

Marlene knew she'd never get to work on time now, and she
hated coming in late. She used to get annoyed with people who
always had an excuse for not being on time. Now, she only had
one excuse. "Danny, where are you?"

"In here." Danny had dumped the race cars onto the living
room floor.

"What are you doing? I told you to wait by the door."
Marlene's stomach tightened as her voice rose. "Sit down." She
forced her son's shoes onto his feet. "Hurry up and get into the car."

Finally, Marlene dropped off Danny and headed for work,
relieved that she could take a break from kids.

Later that day, Marlene arrived at the preschool to pick up Danny and watched the class for a few minutes. The children seemed happy and content, and Mrs. Fithian calmly interacted with them as they cleaned up the classroom.

Mrs. Fithian asked Danny to put away a puzzle. Without any fuss or complaint, he picked up the pieces, plopped them into the box, and slid it back on the shelf.

Marlene's mouth dropped open. Danny obeyed—certainly more quickly than he ever did at home. In fact, Mrs. Fithian gave a few more instructions to him and the other kids, and they listened and obeyed right away. *How can she be so cheerful and get all these kids to cooperate like that?*

Marlene opened the door. "Hi, Mrs. Fithian."

"Hello. How are you doing this afternoon?"

"I really appreciate the way you interact with the children," Marlene began. "Danny responds well to you. Do the kids always listen to you like that?"

Mrs. Fithian smiled. "Well, it didn't start out this way. It took a few weeks for them to learn that I mean what I say. Now they know I only say things once, and if they don't respond, there's a consequence. It took a lot of work those first few weeks, but as you can see, the children are happy when they understand our classroom rules and know that my Action Point is pretty tight."

"Your Action Point? What's that?"

"An Action Point is the moment when I stop talking and start acting." Mrs. Fithian picked up a stack of art papers and began putting them into the children's cubbies. "Many parents are frustrated with their children for not obeying, but in essence they have taught them that they don't have to obey quickly. A tight Action Point is a tool I use to teach obedience."

"I'm not sure I understand."

"Let me ask you something. If you tell Danny to get ready for bed and he doesn't do it, what happens next?"

"I tell him again."

"Then what?"

"Usually I have to tell him three or four more times."

"Does he obey then?"

"No. I usually have to raise my voice next. I don't like to, but it seems that I have to get angry and yell at him before he takes me seriously."

"By giving Danny several chances, you've taught him that he doesn't have to obey you the first time." Mrs. Fithian grabbed another pile of papers. "I know from our previous discussions that you're trying to follow God's principles in raising your family. The Bible gives many helpful insights for family life. I like Matthew 5:37, which says, 'Let your "Yes" be "Yes," and your "No," "No."' In that passage, Jesus taught that extra words are not needed to validate our statements. We should mean what we say when we say it. I think we can apply this to our interaction with children. Danny needs to know that you mean what you say without your having to yell or repeat yourself."

"But I tell him that he should obey me the first time."

"Yes, parents often say that, but do you really mean it?"

"Of course."

"Then why do you give several warnings or tell him so many times? Why don't you follow through with a consequence right away?"

"I never thought about it that way." Marlene paused. There was something here that she needed, but she wasn't quite sure what it was. "Are you saying that I've taught Danny that he doesn't have to listen to me right away?"

"Exactly." Mrs. Fithian smiled. "A tight Action Point teaches children to obey your first instruction."

Marlene glanced at her watch and realized that she needed to hurry in order to meet Jennifer's bus. "Mrs. Fithian, you've given me something to think about. Thanks for sharing this Action Point idea with me."

"Well, having a tight Action Point doesn't solve all the problems, but it does help quite a bit. I've learned a lot by working here and raising my own kids. If you want to talk some more, give me a call and we can set up a time."

"Great! I'd really like that. Thanks again." Marlene took Danny by the hand and led him out the door.

That idea makes sense, Marlene thought as she drove home. *Danny waits to obey until I say something three or four times, yet he responds to Mrs. Fithian right away.*

Later that afternoon, Marlene stood in the kitchen cutting carrots and peppers for the salad. Her thoughts returned to Danny's teacher and the tight Action Point.

Seeing her son's coat on the kitchen floor, she called, "Danny, please come get your coat and hang it up on the hook."

No response.

Marlene could see the kids playing on the floor in the family room. She knew he could hear her, but he wasn't moving. *I'll bet he'd move pretty quickly if Mrs. Fithian gave the instruction.*

Marlene thought again about the Action Point idea. *Just yesterday, Craig asked the kids to help him clean up around the house after dinner. And they did, without complaining or arguing.*

Last week, she remembered, her brother, Patrick, took the kids to the park near their house. When it was time to leave, she had walked up to meet them. Patrick had called the children and, although a bit reluctant, they came running. Surprised, she knew that if she had called them, the picture would have looked different. Patrick had a great relationship with the kids, and when he gave an instruction, they listened. If they didn't, he became quite firm with them.

In contrast, Karla, the babysitter, often had trouble with Danny. Each Wednesday evening, Marlene and Craig went to their small-group meeting at church. This past Wednesday, as they were getting ready to leave, Karla told Danny several times to stop jumping and being wild. He just ignored her. Craig had to step in and speak to Danny.

Marlene's thoughts snapped back to the present as Jennifer yelled from the family room, "I'm telling Mom!"

"You make me so mad!" Danny shouted.

Marlene turned off the stove, Danny's words replaying in her mind. *You make me so mad!* Those were the very words she used when she was frustrated with them. *Is that how I sound?*

After Marlene intervened, Jennifer went outside to play.

I've got to do something different before they learn all my bad habits. Can I teach them to respond to me before I get angry? What will happen if I tighten my Action Point?

She decided to try a little experiment. She walked back into the family room where Danny sat on the rug playing with Legos. "Hey, buddy, come hang up your coat," she said quietly.

Then she slipped out of the room and peeked around the corner. Danny continued to play as if he hadn't heard. "Danny," she called calmly, "if you don't hang up your coat right now, I'm going to send you to your room."

Danny added another section to his tower, ignoring her warning. So she calmly returned to the family room. "Because you didn't obey, you need to go to your room."

Danny looked up, surprised. "But, Mom!"

"No, you didn't obey. Go to your room now."

Danny knocked over the tower and stomped down the hall.

After several minutes, Marlene walked into Danny's room to

find him lying on his bed. She sat down next to him. "Why didn't you obey me the first time I told you to hang up your coat?"

"I don't know." He didn't look up.

"I think I know why. I usually tell you to do something over and over again. But that's not good. It makes you think you don't have to obey me right away. From now on, I'm only going to say things once, and I want you to obey the first time. Do you understand?" Marlene put her hand on Danny's back.

"I guess." He rolled over and sat up.

"God has given me the responsibility to teach you to obey. I'm trying to learn how to do the right things as a mom, and I want you to learn how to do the right things as a child. We need to work together in order to be the kind of family God wants us to be. Does that make sense?"

Danny nodded, and Marlene gave him a hug. "Let's try again. I'd like to see you obey me and pick up your coat."

"Okay." He grinned and headed out the door.

Wow! Marlene thought. *I got through that whole episode without getting upset. I like this new way of working with Danny. Tightening my Action Point can help him learn to obey more quickly and help me stop reacting with anger.*

USING TOOL 1: A TIGHT ACTION POINT TEACHES PROMPT OBEDIENCE

A tight Action Point teaches the value of obedience. You don't develop a tight Action Point just so that you can boss your kids around. There's much more at stake here, and it has to do with character. If your children learn to obey, they'll develop significant qualities that will carry them into successful adulthood. Part of a child's job description is to learn to obey. In the same way that an effective boss gives a list of goals and objectives to employees, children have things they need to learn and do as well.

When we counsel with children in our office, we like to

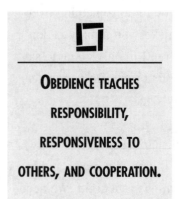

OBEDIENCE TEACHES RESPONSIBILITY, RESPONSIVENESS TO OTHERS, AND COOPERATION.

ask, "What would you think if the mail carrier picked up trash around the neighborhood?"

"Oh, that would be nice," kids usually say.

"But what if he wasn't getting the mail delivered?"

"Oh, then he'd get fired."

"That's right," we say. "He has a job to do: to deliver the mail. That's what he needs to think about. Did you know that you have a job to do? You need to focus on the job that God has given to you as a child—obedience."

Children have a job description, and learning obedience is at the center of it. In fact, God instructed children in Ephesians 6:1, "Children, obey your parents in the Lord, for this is right." God gives children the assignment to learn obedience at home because hidden within this quality are principles kids need in order to be successful in life. When children learn obedience, they learn to give up their agenda for someone else. They become skilled at doing a job without being reminded. They recognize the need to report back when they're done. In short, obedience teaches responsibility, responsiveness to others, and cooperation—three character qualities that will strengthen children and prepare them for adulthood. Parents can teach obedience in a number of ways, but one helpful tool is using a tight Action Point.

How often have you told your child to get ready for bed and then had to say it again and again before he or she started to move? Or have you told your child to pick up toys and then found them still spread all over ten minutes later? How long does it take for your teenager to get off the phone or mow the lawn?

It's easy to get pretty attached to the ways in which you relate to your children, even when those ways create part of the problem. Improving your children's responsiveness often requires adjustments in you before they will make positive changes.

Step 1: Recognize the Cues You Use to Tell Your Children It's Time to Obey

The way you relate to your child is often just as important as what you say. You can change a diaper gently or in a rough way. You can put a child to bed as an item on your to-do list or with loving care. When it's time for your teenager to take out the trash, you can ask pleasantly or harshly. The difference is more than just words. The actions you use and the tone of your voice also communicate a message.

These cues reveal something to your children about your Action Point, the point when you stop talking and start acting, the point when the children know you mean business. *I always mean what I say*, you may think. But children know the difference between the first time you say it and the last time, just before you do something about their lack of responsiveness. A tight Action Point moves your action closer to the first instruction, teaching the children that when you say something, you mean it. How do they know? You give them verbal and nonverbal cues that

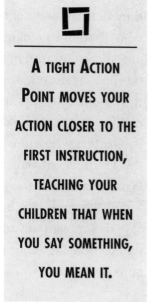

A TIGHT ACTION POINT MOVES YOUR ACTION CLOSER TO THE FIRST INSTRUCTION, TEACHING YOUR CHILDREN THAT WHEN YOU SAY SOMETHING, YOU MEAN IT.

reveal what you're really thinking and meaning. Perhaps you get out of the chair or start moving toward the kitchen where you keep that special utensil. Maybe you raise the pitch or volume of your voice, or use the child's middle name.

If you don't know the cues that tell your kids when it's time to obey, ask them. "I've noticed," you might say, "that I have to tell you several times before you respond to me, but then you do. How do you know when I mean business?" It's surprising how insightful kids are.

One dad said, "I know now that my Action Point has to do with my intensity. Somehow my children learned that when my voice gets loud, they better get moving. I didn't even real-ize it until I began to watch *when* my kids actually responded. I started experimenting and saw that if I increased my volume the first time, they listened. I was shocked. I'm not sure I want my intensity to be the signal, but I now understand what my kids have known all along: I'm giving them cues to know when I'm serious."

The important thing about an Action Point is that it helps children understand when they must obey, and they know that they don't have to obey until then. Furthermore, each person who disciplines children has different Action Points. The rules are a little different in the classroom, for example, than they are on the playground or in the home. That's why when Dad says it, the child may jump into action, but with Mom that same child may not respond as quickly. Kids may take advantage of babysitters who often have loose Action Points.

Think about what it was like in your family growing up. What were the cues your mother or father used that let you know that you had better obey? "They used my full name." "My dad moved toward me." "My mom just gave me that look, and I knew I'd better do it." These are the types of cues we're considering.

What is the interaction like in your family today? If you were able to watch the patterns you and your children have developed, what would you see?

Step 2: Eliminate Negative Cues

For many parents, anger is a primary Action Point. Dad or Mom gets angry, and kids get moving. A raised voice or angry look communicates that action is imminent. Anger, however, can be a destructive emotion, causing more damage than good to the relationship. The trade-off isn't worth it. You may get prompt obedience by yelling at your kids, but you lose the closeness that's possible in your family.

Sometimes a mother will say to us, "You don't understand my kids. They won't respond unless I get angry." We believe she's right, but her children respond that way because she has trained them to. Her kids wait until they see her anger before responding.

Allowing anger to motivate your Action Point is a short-term solution. It says, "I want to solve this problem right now, and I don't care how it will affect our relationship." The parent who uses anger is a bit like the foolish woman in Proverbs 14:1: "The wise woman builds her house, but with her own hands the foolish one tears hers down." It takes intentional work to move away from anger to more productive cues, but you will achieve better results, your children will be happier, and you will preserve your relationship.

Your anger isn't all bad, though. When you become angry at your children's lack of obedience, we suggest that you use your anger as a flag to remind yourself that your Action Point

ANGER IS GOOD FOR IDENTIFYING PROBLEMS, BUT NOT GOOD FOR SOLVING THEM.

is not tight enough. You've allowed a situation to progress far beyond where it should be, and your anger has finally motivated you to take action. The next time you get angry with a child, step back and ask yourself, *Is this one of those times when I should have taken action sooner?* Anger is good for identifying problems, but not good for solving them.

Once you've determined that you no longer want to respond in anger, you can choose new motivational cues. Think of some consequences that can provide the motivation instead of your disapproval or intensity. You might say to a five-year-old, "I've told you once to get your pajamas on. If you don't respond right now, I will pick you up and dress you myself." Or say to ten-year-old Jimmy, "If you don't come in right now, you're going to have to go to bed a half hour earlier tonight."

Step 3: Explain Your New Action Point to Your Children

The next step is to explain the new plan to your children. You don't want to surprise and confuse them; you want to train them. An Action Point determines the rules of the game for parent and child. If you try to change an Action Point without explanation, your children may feel hurt and resentful. Although you have never clarified it before, you have taught your children to respond the way they do. If you're going to change the rules, talk to your children about what you're doing. They will learn to respond to your Action Point as well as to the Action Points of other people.

IF YOU'RE GOING TO CHANGE THE RULES, TALK TO YOUR CHILDREN ABOUT WHAT YOU'RE DOING.

One single mom had a meeting with her two boys, ages nine and eleven. "Boys," she said, "I see a pattern in our relationship that needs to change. I think that I've taught you to respond slowly when I give you an instruction. I now know that God expects you to respond quickly. From now on, I'm going to ask you only once to do something. If you don't respond, I'm going to act with some kind of consequence. This may be a difficult pattern to change for all of us, but it's very important for you to develop the character quality of obedience."

Just as in the earlier illustration, Marlene needed to explain her new Action Point to Danny, you need to do the same. In fact, if you are married, both you and your spouse need to do this. If Mom works hard to teach the children when to obey, this will do little to change their responsiveness to Dad. He must do his own work to teach the kids his cues for his Action Point and the responses he expects.

Step 4: Train Yourself to Respond to Disobedience More Quickly

A tight Action Point means that you will give an instruction, sometimes offer a warning, and then immediately follow through. Don't give an instruction, then a warning, warning, warning, warning, warning, warning, and finally explode. Children know these relational patterns. It's like a game, and they know how to play it better than we do.

So, when you start tightening your Action Point, don't give instructions ten minutes before it's time to eat. You may give your child a warning that dinner will be in a few minutes, but don't give the instructions to wash hands until it's actually time to do it.

Train yourself to respond to disobedience more quickly by giving cues when you want action. It will take some thoughtfulness and self-discipline on your part, but the work you do here will be worth it. If you want your children to be self-disciplined and respond to your instruction the first time, then you need to be self-disciplined and tighten your Action Point.

This tip is particularly helpful for single parents. We know that single parents usually have even less time and energy for repeating instructions and trying to persuade their children to obey. Some parents are so tired by the end of the day that they fall into the trap of not following through at all. Unfortunately, children then learn that they don't have to respond to Mom's or Dad's words and just ignore the instruction.

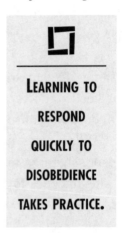

LEARNING TO RESPOND QUICKLY TO DISOBEDIENCE TAKES PRACTICE.

One dad asked his nine-year-old daughter, Denise, several times to come down from the den to clean up the patio. He raised his voice and made several more pleas, but she continued to watch TV, saying, "In a minute," or "I'm coming," with her eyes still glued to the TV.

Finally, he went to the den and clicked off the TV.

"That's not fair!" Denise exclaimed angrily.

"What do you mean 'Not fair'? I must have asked you six times."

She looked up at him, "Yeah, but how do I know when you really mean it?"

Few children are that honest, but that's what's really going on inside their heads. They are simply thinking, *I think Dad [or Mom] is going to want me to come downstairs soon. I can tell because he's mentioned it a few times. I need to be on the lookout so I know when he really means it.*

Learning to respond quickly to disobedience takes practice— for you *and* your child. Practice is important. Give children many opportunities to obey as they're learning the new Action Point. Practice in places and at times when you can work through the process. During our seminars, we're often asked "the grocery store question." It usually goes something like this:

"What should I do if my child acts up in the grocery store?" Using an Action Point well is a skill that requires practice, but it's best to practice in controlled places. The grocery store isn't the place to practice. It's the final exam. If you practice enough at the park and at home, your children will respond properly in the difficult places, too. Children need to see what the changes are and that they're truly going to last.

Step 5: Use Your Action Point Regularly and Consistently

Children will occasionally test your Action Point to see if it's still in place. Don't disappoint them. Firm boundaries provide security. We sometimes find that children obey quickly at home, but don't listen out in public. They sometimes believe that the rules of the game are somehow suspended outside the house. They've been watching, and they know that their parents, for one reason or another, won't follow through right away. In public, their parents use sweet voices instead of the firm ones that work at home, or the parents give several warnings when others are around instead of disciplining right away.

Don't let the fact that you're in public deter you from enforcing a tight Action Point. It's worth it to stop what you're doing and teach obedience. You may feel uncomfortable or even a little embarrassed, but it's important for both you and your children to learn how to respond in any environment.

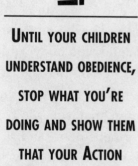

Until your children understand obedience, stop what you're doing and show them that your Action Point is tight no matter what the circumstances may be.

The telephone may be another indicator to your child that rules of the game are temporarily suspended. One mom said, "When I get on the phone, my children fight or get wild. My son complains and whines in ways he never does otherwise." It's amazing how smart kids are. They know if their parents will respond more slowly when on the phone. It's a great opportunity to test the limits to see what Mom or Dad will do.

The solution during these moments, of course, is to teach children that obedience training is more important than looking good in public and more valuable than finishing a phone conversation. Until your children understand obedience, stop what you're doing and show them that your Action Point is tight no matter what the circumstances may be. If obedience is important to you, it will become important to your children also. So be consistent with your children in using Action Points. It's hard work, but your family will reap many benefits in the end.

Step 6: Offer Deserved Praise Liberally

As you work on your Action Point, remember that a tight Action Point works in a positive way, too. Immediate praise for work well done is very motivating. Offer much praise to a child who obeys quickly. It's very important to catch children doing the right thing. Not only do you want to affirm behavior, but you want to encourage the character development that you see. Use phrases such as "You're becoming very obedient" and "I like the way you're learning to obey." Praise goes a long way in building good habits.

In some families, kids learn that if they wait long enough, Mom or Dad will sweeten the deal with some kind of bribe. After repeating an instruction several times, Mom might say, "If you get in the car quickly, I'll let you choose the music we listen to." Or, "If you come to dinner now, you can watch a video later." Or, "If we leave the park now, we'll go get some ice cream." Why would children obey the first time when they know that waiting will bring some kind of reward?

There's nothing wrong with anticipating positive benefits, but if that's the only way you can motivate your children to action, you are not teaching them obedience. You are simply encouraging their selfishness by promising another benefit if they do what you want them to do.

A TIGHT ACTION POINT IS A WAY OF ALLOWING LIFE TO TEACH THE DIFFICULT LESSONS THAT BRING ABOUT CHARACTER IN A TEEN'S LIFE.

Applying Action Point to Specific Challenges

Teenagers

The concept of an Action Point is important for teenagers, too. As children get older, discipline changes. Teens are in that God-given stage when they are choosing values and applying them to life. For this reason, teenagers often need more dialogue and fewer demands. Does that mean that a tight Action Point is only for young children? No. A tight Action Point is helpful for the teen who can't keep his word, is lazy, or is irresponsible.

A tight Action Point is a way of allowing life to teach the difficult lessons that bring about character in a teen's life. For example, if your daughter is ignoring her responsibilities or being unkind to others in the family, she needs to experience the consequences of her actions. After all, a boss won't tolerate rudeness or disrespect. If we're preparing our children for life, why should we tolerate this in our homes? A tight Action Point helps teens grow up more quickly and address weaknesses that are hindering their success.

Divided-household Parenting

Single parents are often frustrated by the fact that the other parent disciplines differently: "My son goes away for the weekend, and it takes him several days to recover when he returns." (Actually, it's not just a single-parent problem. Sometimes parents in traditional families say the same thing: "I do well with my daughter during the day, but when Dad comes home, things tend to fall apart.") A number of factors contribute to this dilemma, but a tight Action Point can be part of the solution. Because kids learn how to respond to each adult, you are not dependent on another parent's actions in order to build healthy routines with your children.

Ideally, it's best for both parents to discipline their kids in a similar way. But when that isn't possible, the extra effort you spend developing correct patterns of relating with your children will pay off. It's especially helpful in these situations, though, to explain why you respond the way you do. In the face of accusations of meanness or strictness, you might say, "I am making choices about how to relate to you, and I choose to respond this way because I know what will make you successful in life. I'm trying to teach you how to obey because, when you learn obedience, you learn many other skills that will help you to be a successful person. I'm not just disciplining you because you irritate me or to get a job done. I'm disciplining you because I want you to develop the character you need as you get older."

Helping Your Children Obey Others

After your children have learned to obey you, take time to teach them how to obey others. Your instructions have become clear cues that you mean business, and your children know it. Unfortunately, other adults don't always know how to give instructions. Attempting to be kind and gentle, for instance, they may give instructions that your children perceive to be suggestions. One mom said, "The Sunday school teacher told me that my son wouldn't obey her when it was time to clean up or line up. I stood by the door and watched the next week, and I realized why. The teacher would say, 'Jerry, can you clean up now?' or 'Jerry, would you like to line up at the door, please?' I realized that Jerry was hearing these as options, not as instructions."

In this case, Mom sat down with Jerry and explained what she saw. "Jerry, Mrs. Mathers feels like you don't obey her at Sunday school. I can see that she has a different way of telling you what to do. Here's what I want you to do. When Mrs. Mathers says, 'Jerry, do you want to come over to circle time?' what you need to hear is me saying, 'Jerry, come over to circle time now.' You need to learn to obey Mrs. Mathers even if she gives instructions differently than I do."

Mom could try to change Mrs. Mathers, but this is a great opportunity to teach Jerry more about following instructions. He needs to understand that different people do things differently, and he needs to recognize an instruction even if it's disguised as a question, suggestion, or opinion. Once you've worked on creating a tight Action Point in your home, your children will be able to transfer what they've learned to other places.

It's Worth It

A child's job description is to learn obedience. Your job as a parent is to teach it. It takes time and effort, but it's well worth the sacrifice. As you work to tighten your Action Point, you can now see acts of disobedience as significant opportunities to teach your children about self-control and responsiveness to authority. Teaching obedience is important, and a tight Action Point is a great place to start.

Here's a quick summary of Action Points:

☐ An Action Point teaches children when they must obey.

☐ Action Points vary among people who discipline.

☐ Children learn to respond to each person's Action Point.

☐ Being consistent with a tight Action Point is hard work, but it's worth it in the end.

☐ There are six steps to creating an effective Action Point.

1. Recognize the cues you use to tell your children it's time to obey.

2. Eliminate negative cues.

3. Explain your new Action Point to your children.

4. Train yourself to respond to disobedience more quickly.

5. Use your Action Point regularly and consistently.

6. Offer deserved praise liberally.

Chapter 2

Making Every Discipline Time Constructive

Marlene walked quickly down the hall. In theory, their morning routine allowed plenty of time for everyone to get everything done with several minutes to spare. The reality, however, was quite different. She glanced into Jennifer's room. *Oh no! Where is Jennifer?*

Marlene hurried into the living room where her daughter sat playing with a new puzzle at the coffee table. "Jennifer, you didn't make your bed or pick up your pajamas." Marlene peered anxiously out the window, looking for the school bus.

"Oh yeah, I forgot." Jennifer tried another piece. "I'll do it in a minute."

"You forgot! You know you're supposed to do those things before you go to school. Now it's time to leave. The bus will be here any minute."

"Can't I just finish this one part?"

"No. You're going to miss your bus. Get your lunch from the kitchen."

Jennifer reluctantly got up and left the living room.

The same thing happens every morning. I can't believe she does this to me.

Jennifer grabbed her backpack and coat.

"You're always dawdling, and this is what happens! If you

can't get everything done in the morning, you'll have to go to bed earlier!"

"That's not fair." Jennifer stomped toward the door, her eyes filling with tears.

"You waste too much time in the morning!" Marlene pushed Jennifer's arm through her coat sleeve. "It's too late to talk about this now." Jennifer ran to the bus stop, wiping away tears.

Marlene watched her and sighed. *There's the school bus. She'll barely make it again today.* Marlene had mixed feelings. Yes, she was relieved that Jennifer would make it to the bus on time. *But why do mornings have to be like this? Jennifer doesn't have that much to do. If she would just concentrate and get those things done, we wouldn't have this problem.*

A loud crash jolted Marlene back to the present. Danny stood in the middle of the family room next to lamp pieces scattered all over the floor.

"Danny! What happened?"

Danny looked at his feet and mumbled, "I don't know."

"What do you mean you 'don't know'? What happened?"

"The ball hit it."

"What are you doing playing ball inside? Take that ball out to the garage right now, and find something else to do!"

Danny picked up the ball and shuffled away.

Marlene stared at the mess, her face flushed. With disgust, she huffed into the kitchen to get the broom and dustpan. As she swept up the pieces, she replayed her anger. *If Danny would just listen and do the right thing, we wouldn't have these problems. I can't believe I have to say the same things over and over. I hate this! It's a battle every day.*

That afternoon, Marlene's neighbor, Bridget, stopped by. Sitting down at the kitchen table, she asked, "How're you doing?"

Marlene looked at Danny in the other room concentrating on his train track, then poured hot coffee into their cups. "I'm okay, but it's been a hard morning."

Marlene enjoyed talking with Bridget several times a week. She and her husband, Bill, and their two children, Chrissy and Justin, lived three doors down. "I'm sorry to hear that. What happened?" Bridget, a sympathetic listener, encouraged Marlene to share.

"Jennifer is so slow in the morning and is never ready when it's time to catch the bus. Today she left her room a mess and didn't make her bed."

"So what'd you do?"

"I was pretty hard on her. We both got upset."

"How'd you leave it?"

"Not too well. She was crying when she left, and I'm still frustrated."

"Oh, that's too bad. Poor Jennifer."

"Poor Jennifer? What about me? If she would just do what she's supposed to do, we wouldn't have this problem."

"Yes, you're right. I was just thinking about Jennifer. It seems as if she had a bad morning, too."

"I guess you're right. Then Danny broke a lamp with his ball, and I completely lost it with him."

"Ouch. I can see why you had a hard morning."

"I don't like getting angry with the kids, but I don't know what else to do."

"I know what you mean. A couple days ago, Justin dug with his truck in my flowerbed and broke some of my flowers. I got angry and yelled at him. We both ended up feeling bad, and the atmosphere around our house was pretty grim. Later, I realized I could do something about it by using a new strategy Bill and I recently learned."

"Really? What is it?"

"Whenever Bill and I discipline the kids now, we've decided to bring some kind of closure by having what we call a 'Positive Conclusion.'"

"What do you do to end positively?" Marlene held an open tin of cookies toward Bridget.

"Thanks." Bridget placed a cookie on her napkin. "We learned to ask three questions and give one statement."

"You always do the same thing?"

"Well, not always, but we usually cover the same ground each time. I regretted not doing this with Justin the other day, so later I found him and we talked about it."

Marlene's curiosity increased. "What are the questions?"

"The first one is 'What did you do wrong?' We want to make sure our kids understand why they're being disciplined. When I asked Justin, 'What did you do wrong?' he answered, 'I played in the flowerbed.'"

"Okay, that makes sense."

"The second question is 'Why is that wrong?' When I asked Justin this, he said, 'Because you told me to stay away from the flowerbed.' Then I clarified it for him. 'You're right. You weren't obeying.'"

Bridget took a sip of coffee before continuing. "The third question is 'What are you going to do differently next time?' I ask this question because I want my kids to think about better ways to handle their problems. Justin answered, 'I'm going to stay out of the flowerbed.'"

Marlene sighed as she bit into a cookie. "You make it sound so easy. I'm not sure my kids will answer those questions."

"Is that because they aren't willing to, or they're not able to?"

"Both. It just doesn't sound like it would work in our family."

"I understand what you mean." Bridget smiled. "It does sound a little forced at first. But I was surprised at how much Justin and Chrissy could figure out. The point is, we're trying to help them learn from the discipline and then end things in a positive way that restores our relationship."

"Well, I do like the idea of ending positively. Some kind of a conclusion like that would certainly help me feel better about the problem."

Bridget leaned forward. "When I saw that Justin was sorry and willing to do the right thing, it was easy to forgive him. We both felt a sense of relief."

"That sounds better than the way I left things with Jennifer and Danny this morning."

"There's one more thing. Bill and I end with this statement: 'Okay, go ahead and try again.' This tells the kids that we believe in them and want them to keep trying. It's like saying, 'You made a mistake, but that's no reason to quit.'"

Marlene shook her head. "All this sounds good, but I'm not sure it would've worked this morning with Jennifer."

"It's hard to discipline when you're in a hurry."

"It might have been better," Marlene said slowly, "to work a little ahead this morning or to save the discipline until this afternoon when she got home from school." Marlene took a sip of coffee. "Do you talk about a problem this way every time you discipline?"

Bridget nodded. "Usually. That's why I felt bad when I got angry with Justin, and then he just went off to play. I think that a Positive Conclusion is important, so I want to get it in somewhere."

"But if Craig and I have a Positive Conclusion, isn't it like saying that what they've done wrong is okay?"

"A Positive Conclusion doesn't replace discipline. It finishes it in a positive way. You'll still have to correct your kids and maybe give them consequences, but a Positive Conclusion helps to clarify a problem and strengthen the relationship. After all, in the midst of the work of discipline, you don't want to sacrifice a close relationship with your kids."

"That's true," Marlene stated.

"Well, I've got to get going." Bridget put her cup in the sink. "Thanks for the coffee and cookies."

"Sure. I'm glad you came over." Marlene gave Bridget a hug.

As Marlene washed the cups and wiped the table, she thought about her interactions with Jennifer and Danny. *Having a Positive Conclusion would be nice. I think I'll try it with Danny.*

Marlene sat down at the table again. "Danny, please come here."

Danny's eyes lit up as he looked at the cookies. "Can I have one?"

"Yes, in a minute. But first I'd like to talk with you about what happened with the lamp."

Danny frowned and shoved his hands into his pockets.

"Danny, look at me for a minute. I just want to talk this through." Marlene reached toward her son to draw him closer. "What did you do wrong?"

"I broke the lamp."

"Yes, but what were you doing that caused the lamp to break?"

"I threw the ball."

Marlene took Danny's hands in hers. "Why is that wrong?"

"I'm not supposed to play ball in the house."

"Yes, that's right."

"What are you going to do differently next time?"

"Play ball outside?"

"Good. That's right, Danny. I'm sorry I got so upset with you this morning. Will you forgive me?"

Danny looked up with a smile. "Sure."

"I forgive you, too. Here, let's each have a cookie."

Later that day, Marlene eagerly watched her daughter walk from the bus stop. "Jennifer, I'd like to talk to you," she said as soon as Jennifer entered the house. They sat down on the couch, and Marlene continued. "I've been thinking about this morning. I'm sorry for speaking harshly to you on your way out the door. That wasn't the best way to handle the problem. Will you forgive me?"

"Okay."

"Let's talk about what happened. Do you know what you did wrong?"

Jennifer fiddled with her ring. "I didn't make my bed and clean up my room."

"That's right. Why is that wrong?"

"I don't know."

"Well, you didn't get all your work done before it was time to leave, did you?"

"No."

"Remember, we talked about what you need to do before school. We each have jobs to do in the morning, right?"

"Yes."

"So you didn't obey, right?"

"I guess so."

"What are you going to do differently next time?"

"I'll make my bed and pick up my pajamas."

DEALING WITH PRESCHOOL CHILDREN

☐ With preschool children, parents can make "What did you do wrong" a multiple-choice question. Most offenses in family life can be boiled down to these three rules: obey, be kind, and show respect. Giving young children a choice between these three rules or character qualities can make this question more productive. As children get older, you can expand their thinking by providing more developed reasons.

"That's good. Try to do better tomorrow, okay?"

Jennifer nodded. "Okay. Can I go play at Cara's house now?"

"Yes, but first you need to make that bed and take care of those pajamas."

"Okay, Mom." Jennifer smiled as she hurried to her room.

Marlene felt a wave of peace. She wasn't sure if it was caused by Jennifer's smile or the look in her eyes, but the Positive Conclusion sure seemed to clear the air.

I feel better. This kind of ending isn't as hard as I thought it would be. They both did okay with it.

USING TOOL 2: A POSITIVE CONCLUSION MAKES DISCIPLINE TIMES CONSTRUCTIVE

Sometimes parents believe that once they've given consequences to their children, the job is finished. They've done their duty and fulfilled their responsibility. Unfortunately, tension often remains. Discipline is not complete until the positive relationship between the parent and child is restored.

A Positive Conclusion is simply a discussion you have with your children after they act inappropriately. The discussion is a debriefing time to clarify the problem, talk about a better response, and restore closeness in the relationship with them. Such a time makes the discipline process a learning experience rather than just a negative punishment. Use this tool every time you need to correct or redirect your children. Talk about the problem and what went wrong; then talk about what could happen differently next time.

Having discussions like this takes a little longer, but it's very effective in helping children to overcome many of their weaknesses. Children can learn to think correctly about mistakes and process offenses in more constructive ways. The Positive Conclusion teaches a mature way of thinking and a way to learn from failures. When children go through the Positive Conclusion, they take responsibility for their actions and learn to be agents of change rather than victims of habit or others' mistakes.

As we saw in the story, a Positive Conclusion after discipline accomplishes many things, but most importantly it helps parents and children keep relational pipes clean and free from hurtful debris. It also encourages repentance and helps children take responsibility for their role in creating problems. Using the Positive

WHEN CHILDREN GO THROUGH THE POSITIVE CONCLUSION, THEY TAKE RESPONSIBILITY FOR THEIR ACTIONS AND LEARN TO BE AGENTS OF CHANGE RATHER THAN VICTIMS OF HABIT OR OTHERS' MISTAKES.

Conclusion, parents can help children develop plans for the next times they face similar problems or temptations. It provides a framework to help children think correctly about mistakes, sins, and offenses. So try to make this process a regular part of your parenting.

You're probably already doing some of the things mentioned in this chapter. That's great. By adding a few more pieces and putting it all together, you can develop a significant tool for change and growth in your kids. Let's explore the Positive Conclusion process a bit more.

Why a Positive Conclusion Is Needed

In many homes, after children experience correction, they continue to feel guilty or, worse yet, plan revenge. True repentance may not take place. This leaves room for anger to linger. Often children don't understand why they received a consequence or what it was they actually did wrong. In order to benefit from correction, they need to understand each offense and also feel unconditional love and acceptance from their parents.

It Helps Children (and Adults) Respond Appropriately after an Offense

Although some children respond well to discipline, many are either blamers or condemn themselves. Blamers can always find someone else who has done something to cause the problem. These children see all of the factors that created the offense except their own. They try to deflect their problems onto their siblings, the dog, or even back onto their parents.

Children who condemn themselves also need to view things differently. Feeling helpless to change, they stay stuck in their problems: "I'm no good. I'll never get it right. Nobody likes me."

One mom said, "My son seems stuck in a rut and is always complaining that he is no good and unlovable. He doesn't even try to change."

Children need to learn to think correctly about offenses. Blaming others or condemning themselves is a poor response. But the problem isn't just with them. Parental anger can also linger. For example, a parent may choose to punish a child by putting distance in the relationship. This is unnecessary and unhelpful. The real benefit comes when the parent and child debrief together and the discipline is completed with a Positive Conclusion.

It Helps to Differentiate Between Punishment and Discipline

The Positive Conclusion can clarify the difference between punishment and discipline. Whereas punishment focuses on past misdeeds, discipline focuses on future good deeds. Punishment looks for justice in order to balance the scales; discipline teaches a correct response and helps children learn wisdom. Punishment is negative; discipline is positive. Punishment is often motivated by anger; discipline is motivated by love. The Positive Conclusion turns what otherwise might be punishment into a constructive learning experience.

How to Make the Positive Conclusion Work

During children's early stages of development (ages two to eight), the structure of three questions and a statement gives children a helpful pattern each time they're disciplined. Although two- and three-year-olds may not initially be able to respond appropriately, it's still helpful to begin this pattern when they are young. You may need to walk preschoolers through the process in order for them to benefit from it. You may even have to answer the questions you ask and have them repeat your words. Children ages four to eight will quickly learn to expect these questions and a statement, and begin to grow from the process. Many parents report that children ages nine to twelve still respond well to the questions.

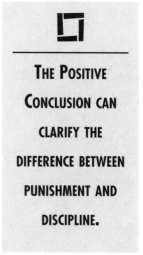

THE POSITIVE CONCLUSION CAN CLARIFY THE DIFFERENCE BETWEEN PUNISHMENT AND DISCIPLINE.

As children grow older, you may need to put aside specific questions and pay more attention to the intent behind them. The principle is the same, though. Teens need to know that a problem isn't resolved until they discuss it with a parent or other person involved.

The Positive Conclusion isn't a time of interrogation. Rather, it's a dialogue during which you and your children can express love, forgiveness, and acceptance. A closer look at the three questions and a statement will show the benefit that each one offers in using discipline times to create constructive learning experiences.

DISOBEDIENCE, CHARACTER WEAKNESSES, AND CHILDISH IRRESPONSIBILITY PROVIDE OPPORTUNITIES TO TEACH YOUR KIDS.

The First Question: Encouraging Confession

Parents discipline their children in a variety of ways and for different issues or problems. Disobedience, character weaknesses, and childish irresponsibility provide opportunities to teach your kids. The Positive Conclusion facilitates the teaching process, and the first question, "What did you do wrong?" helps children take responsibility and prepare to make changes. After all, the first step toward change is admitting there's a problem. This question also gives children healthy patterns to use as they grow older.

Ask, "What did you do wrong?" in a tender way, not accusing your child, but speaking in a matter-of-fact tone. This allows your child to admit his or her personal sin or mistake. If other people were involved (and they often are), a child should not excuse an offense by blaming someone else. The sins or mistakes of others don't justify wrong actions. It's not uncommon for two children to argue and fight, selfishly blaming each other for the problem. "He hit me." "She grabbed my book." Almost always, both children acted wrongly and could have responded differently.

Parents make a common mistake when they dialogue with children about the whole situation: who else was involved, who started it, what else was happening at the time, why these things happen, and so on. Such discussions may be helpful, but it's much better to start by asking, "What did *you* do wrong?" and allow each child to take personal responsibility for part of the problem.

Sometimes children say they don't know what they did wrong. If they truly don't know, it's okay to prompt them. If, on the other hand, they are just trying to avoid responsibility, it's often helpful to give them time alone until they are ready to recognize and "own" their part of the problem. Let's look at the illustration we alluded to above.

"Mom, Bill hit me!" yells Karen from the next room.

"She took my book," Bill shouts defensively.

You walk into the room and try to play Solomon. "Who had it first? Who's had it the longest?" Since Karen is older, she is supposed to be more mature, but Bill has a way of irritating others.

Let's say that you decide Bill should get the book. Disappointed, Karen pouts and says, "No fair." Bill then smirks as if to say, "I win."

What have you accomplished in your little moment of wisdom? Nothing, except contributing to sibling conflict. But what if you put the children into different rooms and tell them, "When you're ready to talk about it, come and see me"?

Bill comes first. "Bill, what did you do wrong?"

"She took my book!"

"I didn't ask you what Karen did wrong. We'll deal with that in a minute. What did you do wrong?"

"I hit her."

Now you've arrived at a significant point in the conversation, because Bill has admitted what he did wrong. Sure, Karen acted wrongly, but Bill needs to deal with his offense and learn a better response to conflict. Although Karen's issues are different, the same approach will work with her. Start by asking the first question, "What did you do wrong?"

Sometimes children say, "I didn't mean it," or "I was only teasing," to dodge responsibility. These excuses rest on the assumption that a person who didn't intend to hurt someone

> **CONFESSION IS A SPIRITUAL ISSUE. NOT ONLY ARE WE TO CONFESS OUR SINS TO GOD, BUT WE'RE INSTRUCTED TO CONFESS OUR SINS TO ONE ANOTHER.**

hasn't done anything wrong. Of course a more mature person recognizes that sins or mistakes, intentional or not, require an apology. So it's important for children to realize and admit their wrong behavior.

Confession is a spiritual issue. Not only are we to confess our sins to God (1 John 1:9), but we're instructed to confess our sins to one another. James 5:16 says, "Therefore confess your sins to each other and pray for each other so that you may be healed." One of the steps toward healing is confession. This is especially true in relationships. Many adults today would find healing in relationships if they could admit their part of the problem. Confession is good at any age.

Unfortunately, many adults still act childishly in this area. They blame, excuse, and rationalize their offenses. Husbands and wives could be more successful in marriage relationships if they would learn to confess their failures to God and to the person they've offended.

The Second Question: Getting to Real Issues

The second question, "Why is that wrong?" addresses heart issues directly. Using it, you can point out negative character qualities such as pride, selfishness, anger, and disrespect. Help your child learn that behavior is only a symptom of something deeper. All of us—parents and children—see outward behavior, but God looks on the heart. If Karen grabbed the book from Bill, she was wrong, but does that mean he can act unkindly? If you were working with each child individually and going through a Positive Conclusion, you could help Bill see that he still needs to respond with kindness and self-control. Karen may be irritated with her little brother, but she needs to realize that's no excuse to be mean. Answering the second question helps to reveal deeper issues that need attention.

At first, most children have a hard time understanding why their actions are wrong. This question gives you an opportunity to gently teach, without preaching, that a particular response was unkind or disrespectful. The word *discipline* means "to teach," and through this question we can help children understand new truths and ideas.

The "why" question and the answers that result provide opportunities for us to teach our children about the ramifications of wrong choices. The book of Proverbs teaches that we are to be a source of insight and discernment. We need to teach that naiveté and immaturity lead people to do foolish things. Actions are foolish when they have unforeseen bad results. We can use discipline times to teach our children to anticipate the consequences of their actions.

YOUNG CHILDREN RARELY THINK THROUGH THEIR CHOICES CAREFULLY AND SELDOM UNDERSTAND ANY REASONING BEHIND THEIR BEHAVIORS.

Sometimes parents confuse this second question with one that is very different in meaning. When a parent asks a child, "Why did you do that?" the child typically answers, "I don't know." This frustrates the parent, who often becomes more intense with the questioning. In reality, younger children rarely think through their choices carefully and seldom understand any reasoning behind their behaviors. Whereas asking a younger child why he or she responded a particular way is usually unproductive, try asking why the action was wrong and help him or her understand the underlying values you are trying to teach.

The Third Question: Planning for Next Time

Once a child realizes why his or her behavior was wrong, the third question helps to clarify what to do instead. "What are you going to do differently next time?" focuses on a better way to respond. The wise parent uses this question to provide training. By talking about the correct response, the child will begin to understand the difference and learn to change accordingly. This usually takes time and repeated discipline sessions.

When using a Positive Conclusion with their children, many times parents will benefit by pausing to ask themselves this question and evaluating what the right action might have been.

Instead of hitting his sister when he's frustrated, what should Bill do? You might suggest that he try to talk to her. If he doesn't get a response that he wants, he can come to you for help. No doubt, he will need time and practice before he's able to change. A Positive Conclusion forces him repeatedly to answer the question, "What are you going to do differently next time?" After saying, "I will talk about it and get help" over and over, eventually he will talk about it and get help.

Many problems our children face are habitual and give us plenty of opportunities to discipline. Unfortunately, many of us miss these opportunities by launching into lectures or yelling at our kids. We become frustrated because we don't see change. ("We talked about this yesterday, and you did it again!") Progress seems so slow. The Positive Conclusion helps children change because it's interactive and involves the children in the correction process. Not only do they learn humility, they also learn solutions they can use next time. These repeated discipline situations cause children to rehearse correct responses repeatedly until improvement results.

One day my (Joanne) eight-year-old son, David, was playing in the neighborhood. He went to an area of a nearby park that was off limits to him without an adult present. Ed and I had given our boys specific boundaries in which they needed to stay, and we usually didn't have a problem. But this particular day, David violated the boundary and went near the water. I knew he had done this because he came back telling stories about a snake and an old snakeskin. I was disappointed. He and I then had a

> **THE POSITIVE CONCLUSION HELPS CHILDREN CHANGE BECAUSE IT'S INTERACTIVE AND INVOLVES THE CHILDREN IN THE CORRECTION PROCESS.**

serious talk about this problem, and I reminded him of the boundaries. He listened and apologized, and I thought that was the end of it.

Unfortunately, later that day I looked for David, and he was nowhere around. I walked down the street just in time to see him coming back over the bridge, leaving his buddy by the water. David had again violated his boundary, this time directly defying me.

I was so sad; my heart ached. "David," I said, "you need to come home with me." We walked home quietly, then had a time of discipline. When David was ready to talk, we had a Positive Conclusion.

We talked about what he had done wrong and why it was

wrong. I used the question "Why is that wrong?" to do some teaching. I addressed the issue of trust—how I wanted to be able to trust him, what trust looks like, and which behaviors show that he is trustworthy. We talked about the privileges associated with being trustworthy and the restrictions necessary when a child is not trustworthy. As we talked, I didn't want to lecture or preach. I wanted him to understand the pain I felt. I wanted to appeal to his conscience.

David began to cry. This wasn't an angry cry of a child being punished, but a repentant cry of a child who was truly sorry he had done the wrong thing. He got the message, and his heart was touched. I hugged him and held him on my lap for a few minutes. I told him that I forgave him. We prayed together. Then I asked, "What are you going to do differently next time?" We then made a plan for the next time he was tempted to go beyond his boundaries. I knew that many times in David's life friends would tempt him to do wrong things, so I wanted him to plan for the "next times." I wanted him to learn the importance of obeying the rules even when no one is looking.

The Statement Ending with Affirmation

Finally, always end with an encouraging affirmation. A helpful statement such as "Okay, go ahead and try again" communicates "I believe in you. Yes, you will make mistakes and sometimes you will even do wrong on purpose. There will be consequences, but we can talk and learn together." Everyone chooses wrong behavior and makes mistakes, and the best response is to stop, think about it, and try again.

The Bible reveals a number of occasions when God or Jesus affirmed the people he disciplined. Adam and Eve, for example, had to leave the Garden, but after stating the consequence, God made them animal-skin clothes and offered them a promise.

The Samaritan woman at the well and David's sin with Bathsheba offer examples of discipline that had positive endings.

After he rose from the dead, Jesus spent time with Peter to reaffirm their relationship (John 21). In the same way that Peter had denied him three times, Jesus gave Peter the opportunity to reaffirm his love three times. After each affirmation, Jesus responded to Peter with a command to do ministry. Jesus commissioned Peter to do the right thing. In essence, Jesus said, "Peter, you chose to do wrong, but I still love you. Go and serve me." Imagine the guilt and embarrassment Peter had lived with. He knew that he had disappointed his Lord, and his conviction caused bitter weeping. Jesus cleared the air and gave Peter the newness of relationship he needed.

Remember the woman caught in adultery who became a victim of the harsh, judgmental religious leaders? (See John 8.) Imagine how she must have looked—sad, dejected, wilting— when they brought her to Jesus. Jesus addressed the Pharisees' problems first, but his gentle handling of the woman is instructive. He said to her the same kind of thing we want to communicate to our kids: "Go, and sin no more." He wasn't justifying her sin; he was giving her a fresh start. His final words to her affirmed her as a person and emphasized that she was competent and capable of doing the right thing.

Likewise, children may need to complete restitution or reconciliation after a Positive Conclusion. Unresolved conflict hinders a clear conscience. A child needs to have the opportunity to say, "I was wrong; please forgive me," and then feel forgiven. The child may need to pick up the book she threw in anger or comfort an offended sibling and then feel that the relationship is restored. This ending doesn't have to take long, but it's important to take a few minutes to bring closure to the discipline time.

Recurring Positive Conclusions

Some parents get frustrated with the Positive Conclusion after a while because their children seem to go through the motions without a heart change. If this happens to you, you may need to use another consequence in order to motivate repentance in your child. However, even if your child is just going through the motions, remember that you are building healthy patterns. God is the one who changes a person's heart, so continue to build healthy patterns and pray that God will do the deeper work in your child's heart. Let's say that your child starts playing rough with the cat again. You might say, "Bobby, that's not gentle. I'd like you to sit down and think about that for a minute. When you're ready, come and talk with me." When Bobby comes back, you say, "Okay, what did you do wrong?"

GOD IS THE ONE WHO CHANGES A PERSON'S HEART, SO CONTINUE TO BUILD HEALTHY PATTERNS AND PRAY THAT GOD WILL DO THE DEEPER WORK IN YOUR CHILD'S HEART.

"I was rough with the cat."

"Yes, you were. Why is that wrong?"

"Because it's not kind."

"Yes, and what are you going to do differently next time?"

"I'll be gentle."

"Good. Go ahead and try again." Bobby leaves to play with the cat, and you're back to your work.

The solution to habitual problems isn't to give one large consequence. Rather, use many small opportunities to have a Positive Conclusion with your child. When you always end times of discipline with a Positive Conclusion, you clear the air and renew relationships. Everyone feels better. The distance or tension is gone because you've talked through the problem. Children shouldn't go around bearing the weight of unresolved conflict or the disappointment of their parents.

Age-specific Tips

Toddlers will not be able to answer the three questions or even understand what a Positive Conclusion means, but you can still start using it early. If a toddler hits you, you may put the child down and say, "No hitting," or "Be gentle," and step back for a moment. Then you may approach him or her again and say, "Are you ready to be gentle? Come here and give me a hug. Let's try again. Here, let me take your hand and put it on my arm. That's gentle." This simple approach becomes a precursor to the Positive Conclusion and prepares young children for a more developed approach as they get older.

Teenagers will probably balk at the use of the three questions and a statement, which may seem childish to them. So the Positive Conclusion may become more of a discussion focused on the same issues. One mom said, "I heard you speak about the Positive Conclusion and thought I'd try it with my seventeen- and eighteen-year-old children. I was surprised that they answered the questions. It worked better than I thought."

Adults sometimes beat themselves up by saying things like "I'll never get it right," or "I'm an idiot." This kind of thinking is just as unproductive as blaming, excusing, or rationalizing faults. We each benefit by asking ourselves, "What did I do wrong?"; "Why is that wrong?"; "What will I do differently next time?" And then saying, "Okay, I'll try again." Processing a problem in this way gives us the freedom to make mistakes, learn from them, and go on to be successful.

It's Worth It

Continue the Positive Conclusion routine because it's the right thing to do, and keep looking for ways to challenge the hearts of your children. One single mom said, "I went through a dry spell with the Positive Conclusion because my son didn't seem to care. But recently, I've seen some indications that he's taking it to heart. I'm glad I hung in there because it's helping us both talk about his offenses and mistakes without anger from either of us."

Here's a quick summary of Positive Conclusions.

- ☐ A Positive Conclusion is a discussion that concludes a time of discipline with
  - clarifying the problem,
  - talking about a better response,
  - restoring closeness relationship with your child.
- ☐ A Positive Conclusion makes the discipline process a learning experience.
- ☐ A Positive Conclusion consists of three questions and one statement:
  - What did you do wrong?
  - Why is that wrong?
  - What are you going to do differently next time?
  - Okay, go ahead and try again.
- ☐ A Positive Conclusion helps the child know what to do right next time.
- ☐ A Positive Conclusion reaffirms the relationship and encourages the child to try again.
- ☐ A Positive Conclusion prepares the way for the child to complete restitution and reconciliation.

Chapter 3

Helping Children Make Lasting Changes

Craig sat at the dining room table putting the finishing touches on his report for the meeting Monday morning. Preparing over the weekend made him feel better.

Marlene looked up from her computer and groaned. "Danny," she called, "it's time for your bath. I've run the water."

Craig knew that his wife wanted to finish up some emails and that Danny's bath was next on the list.

"I don't want to take a bath." Danny flew his toy helicopter around the room.

Marlene continued to work at her computer. After a couple of minutes she looked at Danny and said, "You need to start cleaning up those toys. It's time for your bath."

Danny acted as if he didn't hear.

Marlene walked over to her son. "You need to obey me now and put those toys into the box."

"But I don't want to take a bath."

"Do it now."

Danny threw the helicopter into the box. His frowning face would have been comical in another setting, but not here, not now. Craig could feel the tension as he tried to concentrate.

"No, you don't have the right attitude," Marlene stated. "I want you to start over and say, 'Okay, Mom,' and then do it nicely."

"Oka-a-ay, Mo-o-o-om."

Craig cringed at Danny's whiny tone as the boy picked up the helicopter and dropped it back into the box.

Marlene rolled her eyes. "Just go get in that tub."

"I don't know why I have to take a bath now!" Danny stomped down the hall.

After a few minutes, Craig looked up to see Marlene standing there with a concerned look on her face.

"Craig, we've got a problem."

"No kidding! Danny's attitude's been getting worse the last few weeks." Craig didn't want to get into it just then. "I need to finish this report. Can we talk about this later?"

"Okay, but we need to talk about it tonight. This is a real problem." Marlene walked toward the bathroom.

Later that evening, Craig approached Marlene, who was sitting on the couch reading a book. "Okay, I'm ready to talk about the problem with Danny. You're concerned about his bad attitude, right?"

"Yes, he does what I say, but his heart isn't in it."

"Do you have an idea of what to do?"

"No, I was hoping you had some suggestions. Maybe we have to discipline him more often or take away privileges or something."

Craig sat down next to her. "This reminds me of what Pastor Dave said this morning about the importance of repentance and changing the heart."

Marlene raised an eyebrow, not making the connection. "What? He was talking about church discipline. In the Bible they excommunicated the person who was sinning in order to motivate him to repent. Kicking our son out of the family seems a little extreme, don't you think?"

Craig laughed. "I'm not suggesting that, but Danny needs to repent and change his heart, not just his behavior."

"And how do you think we can get him to do that?"

Craig ignored his wife's cynical tone. "I don't know. There seems to be a big difference between church discipline and family discipline. I wonder what Pastor Dave would say."

Marlene nodded. "Why don't you give him a call?"

"Good idea. I'll try him now and see if he has time to talk." Craig dialed the number. Pastor Dave was more than willing to help.

Craig quickly got to the point. "We've noticed that Danny often obeys but still has a bad attitude. You talked about changing the heart this morning. Any suggestions about how to help *children* change their hearts?"

"That's a great question, Craig. Annie and I are trying to work on that with Nathan and DJ. We want to help them understand that God looks at the heart. That's a very important part of our discipline."

"But how do you do it in your family?"

"We don't want to focus on just their behavior, so we often talk about the heart. We're trying to teach them about their motivations, attitude, and emotions in addition to their actions. Just the fact that we talk about these things helps the boys know that God is interested in heart change, too."

"We had a problem tonight, and we weren't quite sure how to handle it. Danny didn't want to take a bath. He ended up doing it, but he got angry and had a bad attitude. We know we need to encourage a heart change in him, but we're not sure how. Any ideas?"

"It sounds like Danny complied, but you wanted more, right?"

"Yes, that's what I mean."

"One tool we find helpful in those kinds of situations is to have the child take a Break. After Danny's done with his bath, you might have him sit in the hall for a few minutes to think about the problem and his attitude."

"You mean give him a Time Out?"

"Well, sort of. But I don't think Time Out is all that helpful without some goals and purpose. That's why we call it a Break. For example, today when we came home from church, Nathan threw his coat on the floor. Annie asked him to pick it up, and he grumbled. She told him to take a Break until he could talk to her with a good attitude."

"What happened?"

"A few minutes later, he came back and talked with Annie. He admitted what he did was wrong, and it was obvious that his attitude had improved."

"Don't you feel bad sending children away when they've done something wrong? I don't want to communicate that I don't love my kids or don't accept them."

"That's a good point. It's important to do this in a loving but firm way. We're not sending a child away in anger; we're just giving him an opportunity to stop and think about the problem. In a sense, we gave Nathan a Break so he could settle down, reorganize his thoughts a little, and respond more appropriately to what Annie had asked him to do."

"So you don't view this as a punishment, just a chance to settle down?"

"Yes, that's right. In fact, that's the major difference between a Break and Time Out. Instead of a sentence served for wrong behavior, a Break sends the child on a mission to change his heart. We want our children to understand why their behavior was wrong. We want them to *want* to do the right things for the right reasons."

"That seems like a lot to expect from a child."

"It takes time to develop this kind of approach. I'm convinced that only God can change the heart, but we parents can do a lot to prepare our children for God's work. Sometimes they just need to settle down and then come back to the parent and talk about the problem."

"What about giving a consequence?"

"Discipline can be pretty complicated. Sometimes a Break gives children just what they need, and nothing else is required. Other times, though, a child can become quite stubborn, and an additional consequence may be necessary."

"I want to talk to Marlene about this idea. You've given me some good things to think about. Thanks."

Craig hung up the phone and shared Pastor Dave's ideas with Marlene. "I think it would be good if we focused a little more on the heart, not just behavior, with both Danny and Jennifer."

"I like that idea," she replied, "but I'm still not quite sure how it'll all work. We have more control over their actions than we do with their hearts."

"Let's try it and see how they respond. I think the Break will communicate a different message to them. Next time one of them has a bad attitude, let's arrange a Break for a few minutes. Then we'll talk about the heart problem."

Marlene agreed.

The next morning, Marlene saw her chance to try out this new tool. She asked Danny to pick up his pajamas and hang them on the hook.

"Not now, Mom," he replied, heading toward the kitchen.

"Come back here. I want you to do it now, before you eat breakfast."

Danny turned around and huffed back to his room. Marlene watched from the doorway as he hung up his pajamas.

"Okay. Now I want you to talk to me," she said calmly. "The attitude I see shows me that you're obeying on the outside, but your heart is not right. I want you to sit here in the hallway and think about your heart. Come and see me when you're ready to talk about this with a good attitude."

Danny plopped down, and Marlene went to the kitchen to make breakfast.

At one point Danny reached to play with a toy car.

Marlene was watching. "No, you need to sit still and be quiet until you're ready to talk to me."

After about ten minutes, Danny entered the kitchen and stood quietly by the refrigerator.

"Are you ready to talk about it?"

Danny seemed more relaxed; his shoulders were back, and his eyes had a positive look again. "Yes."

Pleasantly surprised, Marlene asked, "Do you understand what you did wrong?"

"I didn't want to hang up my pajamas."

"That's right, and your response showed a bad attitude. It's important to do the right thing *and* have a good attitude. I want to help you learn this. Do you understand?"

"Yes."

"Good. I'm going to give you another job right now to see if you can obey and have a good attitude at the same time. Are you ready?"

"Okay."

Marlene reached into the laundry basket. "I'd like you to take these clean shirts and put them into your drawer."

Danny took the clothes and headed for his room.

Marlene smiled. "I like the way you're obeying, and I like your good attitude."

When Danny returned, Marlene hugged him. He smiled with a sense of accomplishment and bounded over to the table to eat his breakfast.

Well, that went pretty well. A Break helped him change his attitude. I'm going to try this again.

Using Tool 3: A Break Helps Children Change Their Hearts, Not Just Their Behavior

The Bible teaches that God's primary interest is the heart. When Samuel was selecting the first king of Israel, he wanted to choose Eliab, one of Jesse's most handsome sons. But God said to Samuel, "Man looks at the outward appearance, but the LORD looks at the heart" (1 Sam. 16:7). Shortly thereafter, God directed Samuel to choose David, the shepherd.

The wise parent looks beyond a child's behavior to what's going on at a deeper level—the child's attitudes and motivations. The goal of discipline is not only to help children act correctly, but also to guide them into becoming the people God wants them to become. God doesn't just want them—and us—to do the right things. He wants all of us to become the right kind of people.

Many parents work hard to help their children change on the outside. They focus on behavior, so their family looks good in public. Inadvertently, these parents teach their children "image management," the ability to appear good, clean, and nice. When these children grow older, however, and begin to reveal unresolved issues of the heart, their parents are devastated. "What's happening?" they ask. "My children used to be so

THE WISE PARENT LOOKS BEYOND A CHILD'S BEHAVIOR TO WHAT'S GOING ON AT A DEEPER LEVEL — THE CHILD'S ATTITUDES AND MOTIVATIONS.

WHEN WE DON'T ADDRESS CHILDREN'S HEART ISSUES THROUGH DISCIPLINE, THEY RARELY MAKE LASTING CHANGES.

obedient. Now this?" Some of these parents are then frustrated when they realize that their parenting style dealt efficiently with behavior change but not with heart change.

Some children find it easy to connect their actions with heart issues, but most tend to separate the two. They may harbor resentment, selfishness, and/or anger. They may even plan revenge or acts of defiance. Negative consequences seem to only further their trek into negative thinking, eventually resulting in more acting out and misbehavior.

When we don't address children's heart issues through discipline, they rarely make lasting changes. We may feel as if we've done our jobs by giving consequences, but unresolved heart issues linger and fester. If we want our children to grow up to be responsible, godly, mature, and productive adults, we must give attention to their hearts as we discipline. A Break goes beyond behavior modification and provides opportunities for the Holy Spirit to do a deeper work in our children's lives. (See the appendix for more on this topic.)

Why Use a Break

You've probably discovered the futility of trying to teach an unrepentant child or a child caught up in negative emotions. In fact, dialogue during the heat of the moment often makes problems worse, not better. Thus a Break is an excellent way to deal with much of the day-to-day correction children need. It can, in fact, become the primary tool for discipline in a family. The three-year-old who screams out of frustration, the seven-year-old who continually interrupts, and the thirteen-year-old who teases relentlessly all need to understand why their actions are wrong and recognize the need to change their heart attitudes and motivations as well as their habits of behavior. With practice, a Break will give your children a mature approach for addressing heart-related issues.

Even children as young as three or four years old, although not able to understand the word *repentance*, can understand having a soft heart or removing rebellion from their hearts. Older children are able to process some—or all—of what went wrong and come back to the parent with a specific plan for what to do right next time.

At first, children may resist a Break. Some may not want to lengthen the discipline process; they'll try to get it over with too quickly. These children are especially in danger of modifying behavior without repentance. That's why, as we'll explore, it's important for children to learn how to take a Break and make sure their hearts are responding properly before they move to finding solutions.

This is probably a good place to add that we are not suggesting that parents should always use a Break in place of a consequence. In fact, a Break may be used in conjunction with other methods of discipline. We are saying, though, that just administering a consequence and walking away isn't enough. A consequence often doesn't address the heart issues. It may just get the child's attention. Some children can put heart change and behavioral change together, but usually kids

ADMINISTERING A CONSEQUENCE AND WALKING AWAY ISN'T ENOUGH.

need help processing heart issues. Just ask yourself how many times you have corrected your child and come away feeling as if you didn't get anywhere. Something isn't working. Your child is simply not getting the message. A Break helps children change their hearts. Use it often, alone or in conjunction with a consequence.

A Break may just be the beginning. When a child's heart has begun to change and he or she has discussed a particular problem, a consequence is sometimes still necessary. A parent may say, "Tommy, I'm glad you understand why pushing and hitting are wrong. Because you were having a difficult time playing with your brother, you need to play by yourself for a while." Or, "I like the way your heart has changed now. Before you play with Jacob, I'd like you to apologize to your sister." A Break prepares a child to receive correction, understand the consequences of misbehavior, and be willing to change.

When you ask your child to apologize, the best you may get is an "I'm so-o-o-o-rry" with a clearly expressed bad attitude. Even so, don't stop the routine of apologizing. In the same way that cooling Jello becomes firm in a mold, your child is learning patterns for dealing with relationships. Although you may not see a genuine apology, he or she is learning how to respond properly to offenses. Someday, when your child hurts someone's feelings, he or she will want to make it right. At that moment, your child not only will know what to do, but also will have practiced it over and over again, making it easier to offer a genuine apology.

How to Use a Break

Let's explore in more detail how you can facilitate a Break for your children.

Quickly Begin the Break after Misbehavior

When using a Break, remove the child from the situation or activity immediately following misbehavior. You might simply say, "Tyler, that was unkind. Take a Break in the doorway here, and come and see me when you're ready to talk about this." Or, "Sara, that attitude is not helpful. You need to take a Break on that blue chair until you settle down and are ready to talk with me."

Stay Calm

A parent's emotions can turn a discipline time into a volatile argument. It's important for you to remain calm and matter of fact as you progress through the process. This allows the child to focus on the offense instead of on parental anger.

State the Offense and the Directive

Clarify for your child why he's taking a Break. For example, "Hitting is not the way to solve that problem. You need to take a Break." Or, "I don't like the attitude I'm seeing here. Go sit in the hall and take a Break."

Choose an Appropriate Break Location

The best location for a Break is a place away from any activity or stimulation. The bottom step, the hallway floor, or a chair in a quiet room might be appropriate. The actual place isn't as important as the time set aside to change the heart. Some parents send their children to their rooms. Although this may be helpful, for many children, going to their rooms is like a trip to an amusement park. Toys, computers, or other activities easily distract children from the primary purpose of a Break. It's best to choose a boring place where a child can think and is then motivated to return to the parent. A Break place may change depending on your unique situation, but the concept remains the same: the child is sent on a mission to change his or her heart.

Ignore Protests, Excuses, and Tantrums

Some children resist taking a Break and taunt parents into a battle. An angry child wants company and pushes a parent's buttons to invite the parent into a fight. Refuse to join the anger party. Instead, ignore the tantrum and simply say, "We'll talk about it after you take a Break." Don't be distracted by excuses. Children often want to engage you in an argument. A discussion will happen at the end of the Break, but first the child must settle down, change the heart, and be ready to work with the parent.

Don't Take No for an Answer

If a young child refuses to take a Break, pick him up, gently put him there, and say, "You need to obey." You may even hold a child in your lap in the Break to teach this new routine. Simply say, "When you stop fighting me, I'll release my hold." When the child does settle down on your lap, then right away have him sit in the Break alone. For an older child, you may say, "You are not free to do anything else until you take a Break and then talk to me about this."

Don't Talk to a Child Who Is in a Break

When a child returns from the Break, you'll have a dialogue about the problem and a different solution. But while the child is in the Break, don't get sucked into a dialogue. The child's mission in the Break is to change the heart.

THE ONLY PREREQUISITE FOR COMING OUT OF THE BREAK IS THAT THE CHILD IS WILLING TO WORK THROUGH THE REPENTANCE PROCESS.

Allow Enough Time for a Break

The child is told to come back when he or she is calm and ready to talk about the problem. A Break allows the child, under the parent's guidance, to determine when to come back. The length of time a child chooses to stay in a Break is flexible, relating to his or her needs.

The only prerequisite for coming out of the Break is that the child is willing to work through the repentance process. He or she may be ready to change but not know what right behavior to do next time. Remember, repentance is a condition of the heart. Once the child has begun this change, the parent can help the child learn what was wrong and recognize a more appropriate response.

Young children or those just learning how to take a Break may find it difficult to identify what they did wrong, why it was wrong, or even know how to think about the separation. Other children aren't even ready to think because they're too caught up in their emotions. In situations like these, the purpose of a Break is simply to allow the child to settle down and then return to the parent for a teaching time. Frequently, all that's necessary is a reminder, and the child is ready to change the heart and try again. In this case, a Break will be short, perhaps only a few seconds. Other times, because of stubbornness, a change of heart may take longer—twenty minutes or several hours. Either way, encourage the child to initiate the return.

It's important for the child to determine the length of time spent in a Break because it's hard for a parent to anticipate when a child is ready to return or when repentance has taken place. To come back from a Break too soon may short-circuit what God wants to do. To remain too long may cause unnecessary discouragement.

In 2 Corinthians 2:7, Paul encouraged the believers to welcome back a repentant person and not to continue the separation past its intent. He wrote, "You ought to forgive and comfort him, so that he will not be overwhelmed by excessive sorrow."

How will you know when to end a Break? Some children take longer to change their hearts than others. Sometimes children may only settle down while they are alone. Then they can come back and process other steps with the parent. Other times children who are sensitive to God can make significant heart changes during a Break. The wise parent can often discern from the child's face, posture, and tone of voice whether repentance has taken place, or at least that emotions have settled down so he or she can move further in the discipline process.

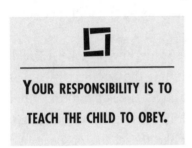

YOUR RESPONSIBILITY IS TO TEACH THE CHILD TO OBEY.

Sometimes children return before they are ready, or defiantly move out of the places where they were told to sit. They just want to get out of the Break and regain their freedom. In this case, you may have to say, "No, I can tell you're not ready yet by your posture and attitude. It looks like you need to stay in the Break longer."

Your responsibility is to teach your child to obey. You must "win" during these situations in order to make a Break an effective tool for discipline.

Remember the Goal

Not surprisingly, children who are upset may respond with a bad attitude when told to take a Break. Stomping feet and slamming doors on the way to a Break must be confronted. When the child returns from a Break, first deal with the initial offense that needed discipline; then give him or her another Break for the continuing bad attitude. You may say something like, "I'm glad we worked out the problem of your fighting with your brother. I think you're ready to play with him nicely. But before you go, we must deal with another problem. I was disappointed that you had a bad attitude when I told you to take a Break. So I want you to take another Break because of that bad attitude. You don't have to stay there long, but I'd like you to show me that you can take a Break with a good attitude." Then have the child practice walking to the Break. When he or she returns, talk about the stomping and slamming and what a good response to correction looks like.

One dad told us about his seven-year-old daughter, Kelly, who was yelling at her brother. Dad called her upstairs to talk about the problem, and she began yelling at him. He sent her to take a Break and settle down. About a minute later, she came back but was obviously not changed. Her head was tilted down, her posture was slumping, and her bottom lip was sticking out. Dad didn't even have to talk with her. He just told her what he saw. "Kelly, I see that you're not ready yet. The way you're standing and the expression on your face tell me that you still have a problem in your heart. I want you to continue your Break until you're ready to come out with a changed attitude."

This time Kelly stayed away for about twenty minutes, and when she returned, she was obviously different. Dad took her head in his hands, looked deep into her eyes, and said, "I can see your heart in there. It looks nice right now. It looks like you're ready to talk about this." Kelly giggled, and they continued to talk about the problem of handling her anger.

If your child repeatedly returns from a Break every few seconds, you may need to establish a minimum length of time. You could say, "Sam, your attitude doesn't seem to be changing, and you continue to come back to me. So I want you to stay in the Break for at least ten minutes. You can stay longer if necessary, but you may not come to me for at least ten minutes. Let's see if that helps."

What do you do if your child will go into a Break but won't come out? Sometimes this is a manipulation, but other times he or she is just unmotivated to return. Keep in mind that the attraction to return is that the child is missing out on some of the benefits of family life. You may remind the child of those benefits and gently coax him or her out of the Break. If the attitude is just stubbornness, you may choose to allow the child to stay there for an extended time. Over time, children learn that a Break is not an elective. It's a required course. Remember that the goal is to help children change their hearts. A Break is one method to help accomplish that goal.

How Do Children Change Their Hearts?

Throughout this chapter, we've referred to children "changing their hearts." A complete change of heart takes a lifetime, but God often uses small, day-to-day changes to accomplish this greater work. Small steps of right thinking and attitude adjustments contribute to lifelong patterns of godliness. Likewise, it would be unreasonable to expect a lazy child to instantly become diligent. So what *do* we expect from a child who takes a Break? Let us share the following illustration.

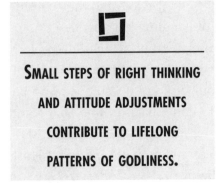

SMALL STEPS OF RIGHT THINKING AND ATTITUDE ADJUSTMENTS CONTRIBUTE TO LIFELONG PATTERNS OF GODLINESS.

One day, when my (Joanne) children were young, I asked them, "What happens in your heart when you take a Break? I see that when you start the Break, you're angry, and when you come back, you're changed."

Timothy (age five) responded, "I think about it, and I'm sad I did it."

David (age seven) said, "I think about what I did wrong, and I feel sorry."

Children may not understand how it happens, but with practice they are able to make heart-level changes. These heart-level changes, or repentance, in children, involve several steps:

WORKING THROUGH A CHILD'S CONSCIENCE, THE HOLY SPIRIT MAKES SIGNIFICANT INROADS INTO THE CHILD'S ATTITUDES AND MOTIVATIONS.

1. Stop doing wrong, calm down, and be willing to talk about the problem.
2. Acknowledge doing wrong— to God and the person who's been offended.
3. Be willing to change.
4. Commit to doing right.

Ideally, two other steps of repentance take place:

5. Feel sorrow for wrongdoing.
6. Have a *desire* to do what's right.

These last two steps of repentance, however, involve a work of God's grace in a child's heart. Parents can't force children to completely change their hearts. Only God can thoroughly transform inner desires and motivations. Children, however, can do a number of things to set the stage for God's work to take place. They can change their thinking, values, and attitudes. They can calm down and acknowledge that they did something wrong.

The Holy Spirit is a key factor leading to heart change in a child. Working through a child's conscience, the Holy Spirit makes significant inroads into the child's attitudes and motivations. A Break slows down the discipline process and gives God an opportunity to work on deeper issues in the child's life.

My Child Isn't Changing

Sometimes a parent will ask, "What if I'm doing all these things, but my child is just going through the motions and her heart isn't changed?" It is true that some children resist change or just want to get through the process and get on with life. Sometimes these children need additional consequences to help grab their attention. Other times, they need a longer Break. Keep in mind that each discipline time contains a teaspoonful of opportunity. Sometimes parents want to put a bucket of truth into an opportunity that can only handle a small amount. A complete change of heart takes a lifetime, so do what you can with this experience and move on. If your child is having trouble in a particular area, you'll be providing discipline here again. Change takes time.

Pray that God will breathe life into the Break routine, and keep using it in your child's life. Parents sometimes make a big mistake by dropping a routine because the child's heart response isn't there. Yet God uses those same routines over time to bring about internal change. So continue the Break even when you experience resistance, and pray that God will do the deeper work of changing your child's heart. The Break is a proven way to build helpful patterns that God can eventually use in deeper ways.

It's Worth It

A Break is an effective tool to motivate heart change in a child. It usually takes some time to develop this routine, but do the hard work, and you'll use it regularly for years to come. Furthermore, your child will grow up learning the value of settling down and making heart-level changes. You may not see significant improvement right away, but keep at it, and over time your child will grow into a person who is able to make a mature response to correction.

Here's a quick summary of how to use a Break:

1. Quickly begin the Break after misbehavior.
2. Stay calm.
3. State the offense and the directive.
4. Choose an appropriate Break location.
5. Ignore protests, excuses, and tantrums.
6. Don't take no for an answer.
7. Don't talk to a child who is in a Break.
8. Allow enough time for a Break.

Break vs. Time Out

	TIME OUT	BREAK
Goal	punishment	repentance
Focus	behavior	heart
Length of Time	determined by parent	determined by child
Role in Discipline	a consequence	part of the training process
Responsible Party	parent has responsibility for the child's reentry	child has responsibility for making changes and returning
Attitude of the Parent	emphasizes distance between parent and child	emphasizes the parent's desire for the child to return

For more information on the differences between a Break and a Time Out, see the appendix.

Chapter 4

Communicating Values so Kids Will Listen

The cabinet floor was painfully hard as Craig lay on his back under the kitchen sink. He scooted in another inch to see if he could get a better view of the leaky pipe.

Danny burst through the doorway. "Jennifer won't stop squirting me!"

Craig scowled as he put down his wrench, wiggled out of the cupboard, and headed to the back door for the third time that morning. "Jennifer! Stop squirting your brother!"

"He asked for it," she called, still holding the dripping hose in her hand.

"Just leave him alone, and find something else to do."

Craig turned and walked back to the sink. "Danny, go back out and play."

Fifteen minutes later Jennifer shouted from the family room, "Dad, Danny keeps shaking my table, and I'm trying to color."

Craig shook his head. "Danny, stop shaking the table!" *I'll never get anything done with all this fighting,* he thought. *Why do they tease each other so much? I'm constantly telling someone to stop this or stop that. I wish they'd have more respect for each other and show a little kindness.*

"I want you two to come here," Craig said, formulating a plan.

Jennifer and Danny appeared in the kitchen doorway.

"I'm trying to get some work done while your mother is at Bridget's, but every few minutes I have to stop and solve your problems. I want you to stop annoying each other and get along."

"But Danny keeps bothering me," Jennifer complained.

"If Danny is bothering you, I want you to tell him to stop. You don't need to call me."

"He doesn't listen to me."

Craig turned to his son. "Danny, if Jennifer asks you to stop, I want you to stop. Do you understand?"

"What if she's bothering *me*?"

"Then you can tell *her* to stop, and she needs to listen to you. Okay, Jennifer?"

"I *do* listen to him."

"I want you both to learn to respect each other's words. I think we'll make that a rule around here. When someone says stop, the other person has to stop. You got it?"

Both children nodded.

"Okay, let me finish up here. You go play." Craig looked through his toolbox for his vise grips.

Marlene arrived home twenty minutes later, just as Craig was putting his tools away. "How'd things go this morning?" she asked.

"All right. I finally finished fixing this sink, in spite of all the bickering between the kids."

"Did they have a hard time?"

"They were irritating each other and kept coming to me and tattling."

"That sounds familiar."

"Well, after stepping in a few times, I got frustrated. I feel like a referee."

Marlene took a deep breath. "I know what you mean."

"I talked to them about it."

"Oh, you did? And what happened?"

"I told them that they need to listen to each other. If they don't like something the other one is doing to them, they can say stop, and the other one has to listen. I told them it's a new rule for our family."

"A new rule?" Marlene raised her eyebrows and looked at her husband. "Did it work?"

Craig could hear the skepticism in her voice. "Well, it's too soon to tell, but I like the idea of having them try to work things out together before they come tattling."

"It'll be interesting to see if it helps. Believe me, I'm open to any suggestions. I'll be happy if they just listen to each other once in a while."

"That's the whole point. I want them to *learn* to listen to each other."

"Don't you think you're asking too much? They're still young."

"Yeah, but if we could teach them to respect each other's words, we'd be teaching them something important. At some point, they've got to learn to work things out and listen to each other."

"I agree with you there. Let's just see what—"

Jennifer rushed into the kitchen. "Dad, I told Danny to stop, but he won't!"

Marlene turned to Craig and waited.

"Danny, come here," Craig called. "Jennifer, you stay here, too. Let's talk about this."

Danny entered the room.

"What happened?" Craig asked.

Jennifer leaned forward, her eyes intense. "We were playing with the dominoes. We were standing them up in a line and knocking them down. Then I wanted to play by myself, but

Danny kept knocking mine down. I told him to stop, but he kept doing it!"

"Is that right, Danny?"

Danny looked at his sister and rolled his eyes. "I was just playing."

"But you didn't stop when your sister said stop, right?"

"Yeah."

"Okay, this is the new rule we talked about this morning. I want you to learn to listen when someone else says stop. Danny, you need to play by yourself in your room for a while."

Danny sighed and headed down the hall. Jennifer went back to the family room.

Marlene gave Craig a cautious smile. "Maybe this will work. I really like the idea of having a rule that teaches them to respect each other."

"One thing still bothers me though," Craig said.

"What's that?"

"Well, the 'Stop' rule, if we can call it that, is okay for teasing and annoying, but what about when they start to argue with each other? What kind of rule can we use to teach kindness and respect when they're fighting over a toy?"

"That's a good question." Marlene laughed. "I never know who had it first or who started the problem. Whatever I decide, somebody complains, 'That's not fair!'"

"We need to think of a way to deal with that, too. I'm sure they could solve more of their problems instead of tattling or bickering about them."

A few hours later everyone went outside to rake leaves. Danny ran toward the shed. "I want the red rake!" he exclaimed. Jennifer got there first and quickly grabbed it.

Danny turned and yelled, "Mom! Tell Jennifer to give me the rake."

"Jennifer—"

Craig raised his hand to interrupt his wife. "Wait a minute, Marlene. *We* don't need to choose who gets the red rake."

Marlene paused.

"What's the problem, Danny?" Craig began as he tried to think of a better way for his son to approach the problem.

"She always gets the red rake," Danny complained, walking closer to his dad.

"I want you to go talk to Jennifer about this instead of complaining to Mom."

"But she won't give it to me."

"Danny, I've got a plan," Craig said, bending down toward his son. Almost in a whisper, he continued. "Go over to Jennifer with a good attitude and say, 'You had the red rake last time. Could I have it today?' Maybe she'll let you use it."

Danny smiled and ran back to the shed.

Craig and Marlene stood watching and listening. *What's going to happen here? Can they work it out?*

"You had the red rake last time. Could I have it today?" Danny asked.

Jennifer looked at Danny and then at her parents watching from halfway across the yard. "How about we take turns? I'll use it first; then you can have it."

"I want it first," Danny said.

"Okay, you can have it for a little while; then it's my turn."

"Okay."

Jennifer handed him the rake and looked over at her parents for approval.

Craig smiled and nodded.

"This is great!" Marlene said. "They came up with a better solution than I would have."

"You're right. I think we should give them more opportunities to solve problems for themselves. I'm sure it won't happen like this all the time, but if we give them some guidelines for solving problems together, maybe they could do more of it on their own."

HOW TO MAKE RULES INTO LESSONS THAT TEACH VALUES

Sometimes parents establish rules first and then search for the corresponding values, but it's most helpful to work from values to rules.

1. Determine the problem that needs to be addressed. Clarify it as specifically as possible.

2. Identify the value that is lacking. Define it simply, in a way the child can understand.

3. Establish a family rule that demonstrates the value.

4. Proceed through the above steps with the child, when possible, to teach the value as well as the rule.

5. Remember that rules change as children grow older, but values and principles remain the same. More values and principles are added during maturity to balance and complete those learned earlier.

USING TOOL 4: FAMILY RULES—CONSISTENTLY APPLIED—TEACH VALUES AND PRINCIPLES

Every family needs rules. Of course an overemphasis on rules can hinder or even eliminate a positive atmosphere around the home. But too many families have moved to the other extreme, trying to eliminate rules altogether. This often results in confused expectations, anger, and disappointment. Rules are values put into action. They're the practical application of what we believe.

Sometimes rules are clearly defined, even posted on the refrigerator or in a hallway. Other times they're not as visible but just as important. For example, Ian knows better than to ask Dad if he can watch the movie *The Return of the Ax Murderer.* He knows that Dad will say no because it's rated R. Ian may focus on the rule, however, without understanding Dad's convictions. That's why it's important for Dad to communicate and discuss the values on which the rule has been established.

The Connection Between Rules and Values

The rule involving Ian and R-rated movies is supported by a number of values. Dad, who knows that violence and gore aren't appropriate for Ian to watch, has already talked with Ian about why his son isn't allowed to watch R-rated movies. That talk was filled with reasons, and most of those reasons were tied to values. The resulting rule summarized the conclusion.

The connection between rules and values is so important that it would be good for you to regularly ensure that

❑ your rules are based on the values you want to teach,

❑ your values are defined clearly through rules,

❑ you frequently communicate the connection between rules and values.

Your values and convictions represent your heart. You are a child of God, and he wants to build within you a heart that's like his. Part of your job as a parent is to transfer your heart— including biblical values—to your kids. You take your kids to church, make sure they complete their homework, and may enroll them in music lessons or sports. Why? Because you know those things will impact who they are and who they will become. One of the best ways to connect with children on a deeper level is to teach them values through the rules of everyday life.

Think for a moment about some of the rules you had to obey as a child growing up. No doubt they were similar to these: "Be in the house by dark"; "Park your bike in the backyard"; "Come straight home after school"; "Don't touch Dad's tools without asking." How quickly they come to mind.

It's interesting to look at rules such as these and ask, "Why did my parents have those rules in our home?" We may not have understood then, but as parents ourselves now, it's not hard for us to recognize underlying values. For example, safety is important at any age, but knowing where to draw the line to limit a child's freedom can be challenging. You might not allow a three-year-old out of the house unsupervised, but your five-year-old can play unattended in your fenced yard, and a teen may stay at a friend's house until seven at night. Each of these guidelines is a different rule based on the child's maturity, but all three uphold the value of safety.

Good Rules Are an Extension of Values and Principles

Good rules show children what family and societal values look like, how to put them into practice, and why they are relevant. Such rules draw lines in life so people know what's expected and how to operate. The lifeguard posts a list of rules in order to define how to play safely at the neighborhood pool. A teacher discusses rules about how to act respectfully in her classroom. Even boys in the neighborhood establish rules for their club by which members must abide.

When my (Scott) children were younger, our household had clear rules about manners during mealtime. We had seven people eating around our table, so we taught our children to say three things if someone wanted something: the person's name, "would you please pass ...," and the item they wanted. Thus, "Give me the butter" was not acceptable because it did not demonstrate thoughtfulness toward others. "Melissa, would you please pass the butter" was the acceptable approach.

GOOD RULES SHOW CHILDREN WHAT FAMILY AND SOCIETAL VALUES LOOK LIKE, HOW TO PUT THEM INTO PRACTICE, AND WHY THEY ARE RELEVANT.

Furthermore, it seemed as if some of our children thought that "amen" was the Greek word for "go." Immediately after the prayer, they grabbed or asked for something. So we established another rule: after the prayer, each person would look for an item nearby and offer it to the next person, saying, for example, "Megan, would you like some green beans?"

One family taught a similar approach in order to encourage mealtime manners. Five-year-old Jack offered a plate of chicken to his three-year-old sister, Cheryl. "Which piece of chicken would you like?"

Not knowing much about the anatomy of a chicken, she said, "I'll take the foot."

Jack, a little frustrated, replied, "Cheryl, a chicken doesn't have a foot. Pick something else."

Cheryl, relishing this attention but still not quite understanding, replied, "Okay, I'll take a hand."

Jack was getting hungrier by the minute, and his patience was wearing thin. "Cheryl, chickens don't have hands. They fly. Pick something else." Mom and Dad were trying to control themselves so as not to burst out laughing.

Cheryl, wanting to be cooperative, thought through the list of body parts she knew, and said, "Okay, I'll take the head."

Jack replied angrily, "Mom doesn't cook the head."

Knowing she better do something fast, Cheryl said, "Okay, just give me the belly button."

Mom and Dad couldn't handle it any longer. They roared with laughter as Jack put down the platter, grabbed a piece of chicken, and said, "Here, take a breast. That's about as close to the belly button as you're gonna get."

Emphasizing a Value Makes a Rule Come Alive

At one point in our family life, my wife, Carrie, and I (Scott) sensed a problem of dishonesty in our home. We had a rule about telling the truth, but Carrie felt as if we needed to emphasize it a little more to prevent the problem from escalating. When we'd find a broken toy or a mess, it seemed that no one would take responsibility for it. Some of these things were hard to prove, so instead of trying to pin children down, we decided to deal with the problem in a positive way.

We spent a couple of weeks talking about what Carrie called "Honesty under Pressure." She talked about the importance of honesty and read stories such as "The Emperor's New Clothes" and "The Boy Who Cried Wolf." She asked us each to tell about a time we chose to tell the truth under pressure—when honesty made us feel embarrassed, or got us into trouble, or we had to apologize. She also developed an Honesty under Pressure award that mysteriously appeared on the bedroom door of a child who told the truth in a difficult situation. This emphasis on the value of honesty made the rule come alive for us and significantly addressed the problem we faced.

Develop and Use Rules Appropriately

Rules, a means by which we teach values and principles, are sometimes overemphasized or misused. For example, some parents focus so much on enforcing manners at the dinner table that they lose the relational benefits of mealtime. (It's been said that more meals are ruined at the table than at the stove.) A careful balance is important. As you develop rules in family life, be careful to use them as opportunities to teach, not opportunities to lecture or criticize.

AS YOU DEVELOP RULES IN FAMILY LIFE, BE CAREFUL TO USE THEM AS OPPORTUNITIES TO TEACH, NOT OPPORTUNITIES TO LECTURE OR CRITICIZE.

Sometimes parents enforce rules without knowing why such rules exist. Perhaps the rules were in place when they were kids but now don't apply. One mom said, "We had a rule at dinner that everyone had to eat all the food on their plates before dessert. My daughter is a little on the chubby side, and I realized that my rule was contributing to her weight problem." After evaluating the rule, this mom realized that it actually went against her values, so she changed it.

IF RULES ARE SEPARATED FROM UNDERLYING VALUES AND PRINCIPLES, CHILDREN MAY VIEW THE RULES AS PRISON BARS TO BE TOSSED ASIDE AT THE FIRST OPPORTUNITY.

What rules do you have in your family? What do they teach? Why do you teach your children not to interrupt someone who is talking? Why is it important to ask permission before borrowing someone else's toy? Why should children put away toys after they've finished playing with them? Behind each one of these rules is a value children can embrace. Take time to talk with them about these values. This discussion makes rules more meaningful, especially for older children and teens.

If rules are separated from underlying values and principles, children may view the rules as prison bars to be tossed aside at the first opportunity. When this happens and rules are abandoned, children may completely miss the underlying values. So, when establishing and enforcing rules in your family, talk about the values they represent.

If you or your children feel as if rules are emphasized too much, go back to talking about values and ways to implement them in family life. Allow your children to help apply values by creating their own rules. Be careful to avoid extremes. Some parents talk about values vaguely and don't teach their children how to relate values to life. Other parents overemphasize rules without teaching the values behind them. Both of these mistakes result in children and parents becoming frustrated.

Motivating children to obey is part of parenting, but by no means is it the end. Teaching values will help children develop wisdom about life. You can teach values in a number of different ways, but one tool for raising wise children is using family rules to teach those values.

Feel free to create new rules in order to teach values you realize are lacking in your family. For example, if your children are mean to each other, you may teach new rules emphasizing the value of kindness. Besides all the don'ts—don't hit, kick, yell, grab, or push—positive demonstrations of kindness can be expressed: You must take others' feelings into account as you make choices and play games; except for rare situations, you should share a toy you are not using; and include other children who want to play. Such rules help children understand how to be kind in practical ways. Look for ways to connect values to rules, and you'll be surprised at how much more cooperation and thoughtfulness you'll receive.

Many of the values and principles you apply in family life actually come from the Bible. It's good to show children ways in which the Bible applies to their everyday lives. Good values and principles exist in the world, but recognizing their biblical basis makes them more powerful and relevant.

GOOD VALUES AND PRINCIPLES EXIST IN THE WORLD, BUT RECOGNIZING THEIR BIBLICAL BASIS MAKES THEM MORE POWERFUL AND RELEVANT.

As parents, we want our children to embrace our values and convictions, so we continually look for ways to persuade them that what we believe is best. Unfortunately, they sometimes resist these values, not yet understanding our convictions and the serious consequences of their actions. In this situation, rules become fences that help to control behavior until these children realize the importance of the underlying values. To use a simple illustration, maybe your parents expected you to keep your room neat. Now, years later, you realize that this rule was designed to encourage cleanliness, organization, and self-discipline, but back then it seemed like an intrusion.

Some parents, when their children misbehave and reject appropriate values and rules, just create and enforce more rules. Although structure and firmness are helpful, we must remember that rules focus on behavior, but God is interested in the heart. Rules can solve problems temporarily, but much more is needed to help children learn to translate those rules into godly values and principles that guide their lives.

Jesus challenged the Pharisees, who invested their spirituality in rules instead of relationship. He called them hypocrites because they measured themselves by their rules and ignored the condition of their hearts.

Sometimes children obey the rules, but their hearts aren't in it. ("Please share your bike helmet with your sister" addresses obedience. "Are you being loving?" addresses a value.) When situations like this arise, be honest with your kids and explain your convictions. Also, be humble enough to acknowledge that there are other ways of accomplishing the goals of family life. Other people may do things differently, but emphasize in loving ways that you believe the best thing for your family right now is to obey this set of rules, which is derived from sound convictions and values. Yes, you'll change over time and so will your kids. It's all part of learning and growing. With your attitudes in the right place, however, your children will learn and retain more than you ever imagined.

Don't let their resistance to your rules deter you. Kids may resist, but they're still learning all the time. As they grow, they'll remember the boundaries you set up. And hopefully, because you've done a good job of communicating your heart, they'll discover that godly values are engraved into the deeper areas of who they are, too.

Young children often have a hard time understanding abstract ideas such as patience or kindness. As you establish rules to teach these abstract concepts, you give your children concrete actions that they can put into practice. Rules put hands and feet on the values and principles you want your children to learn.

As your children mature, they will better understand the concepts behind your rules and more fully embrace the principles you teach. Your work early in your children's lives prepares the way for a deeper understanding later. Later on, they will need fewer specific rules because they have begun to internalize key values. They will make decisions based on principles they learned by living within the boundaries you've created through the years.

Exploring Foundational Values and Principles
God gave two basic rules to children in Ephesians 6:1–3: obey and honor. He knows that hidden within these qualities are the success principles children will need for the rest of their lives. God's rules always contain values! Sometimes these values are obvious; sometimes they're not. But God's values for his children inspire the rules he created for them.

Let's explore some key values and principles that children need to learn, and some rules that help to teach these values.

Three "Starter" Values
It's helpful to simplify the values as much as possible for young children. You may want to start by emphasizing three values that are foundational to family life, values that provide

a springboard for teaching more values later and become the basis for most rules,

□ Obedience.

□ Respect.

□ Kindness.

Responsiveness to Authority

As a parent, you won't get far in the discipline process if you call your son and he runs the other way. So responsiveness to authority is a key value you'll want to teach young children. A helpful rule to teach this is the "Come When You're Called" rule. When children don't learn to come when called, they learn to ignore your voice. Then, not surprisingly, when you get in the habit of yelling instructions throughout the house, your kids find it easier to be unresponsive.

If a young child is two houses away when you want to talk with him, just call his name: "Brian!" Teach him that when he hears you call his name, he needs to come. He shouldn't yell, "What do you want?" If he does, say only his name and ask him to come: "Brian, come here, please." Don't carry on a conversation by yelling. As you teach him to come when he's called, he learns responsiveness to authority. When Brian does come to within a few feet, he should ask, "What, Mom?" or "What, Dad?"

Now you may be thinking, *That's fine for you, but my kids won't come.* Getting your children to come quickly when you call will probably take practice. Let me (Joanne) share with you how I taught this to Timothy when he was two and a half.

First, I explained to him what I expected. I told him that from then on, whenever I called his name he needed to come close and say, "What, Mom?" I explained that since I was his mother, he needed to learn to listen to me. Then, I gave him a chance to practice.

The natural thing for Timothy to do when I called was to yell back, "What?" I had to refrain from answering his question and learn to repeat my request by saying, "Timmy, come here." When Timothy finally came, I would review the rule with him.

I practiced this rule every chance I could. I didn't only want to call him when I needed to discipline him or when he was running away from me in a store. I practiced at home and at the park. Sometimes I would call him to give him a snack, a hug, or just to praise him.

Timothy liked this game. He'd beam from ear to ear when we played it, and I praised him for coming quickly. Sometimes he would initiate the game himself. He'd say to me, "Mommy, call me and see how fast I come." It started as a game for him, but children learn through play. Timothy learned to respond to my authority and developed a sense of accomplishment at the same time.

The Come When You're Called rule lays the groundwork for positive communication patterns as children grow, and teaches responsiveness to authority. Children of all ages need to learn this value, starting at home. A five-year-old learns to ask permission before turning on a video. An eight-year-old leaves the computer game because Dad is calling. A thirteen-year-old follows the instructions of the teacher at school with a good attitude. All of these are examples of children responding well to authority.

Self-discipline

Self-discipline is a key to success, so the earlier children can learn this value, the better. Here's a glimpse into my (Scott) family as my wife and I taught our youngest children the value of self-discipline.

When our adopted twin girls, Elizabeth and Megan, first came to us, they were not self-disciplined. They were four years old but often ran away from us in public places. They were energetic and eager to touch things and explore the world. When we visited someone's home, they would disappear and come back with a prized stuffed animal off someone's bed or a decorative piece off a shelf. It was embarrassing. Knowing that we needed to do something fast, we started using the "No Touch" rule.

I chose to teach this rule at a time that was convenient for me. I explained to the three young children (our biological son, Ben, was also four years old) that when we entered someone's house or a store, they were not allowed to touch anything without first receiving permission. I then announced that I was going to the auto-parts store and invited the children to go with me. All three eagerly accepted my invitation. I reminded them about the No Touch rule and told them that only children who would obey the No Touch rule could go.

I spent about fifteen minutes in that store, mainly supervising my children. I paid attention to them, looking at things they wanted to show me, but they were not allowed to touch anything. Just as I was ready to pay the cashier, I turned around and saw that Ben had taken something off the shelf. "Dad, look at this," he said. Obviously, he had broken the No Touch rule.

"Oh, Ben," I said with sorrow in my voice, "I'm so disappointed you picked that up. Go put it back."

I paid for my merchandise, and when we left the store, we debriefed about the No Touch rule. I told Ben that if he couldn't obey the No Touch rule, I couldn't take him on special trips to the store.

About a half hour later, as is often the case when I'm trying to fix my car, I had to return to the same store. I announced that I was going, and, once again, they all wanted to go. (Young children get great joy out of simple trips to the store. When they get older, you've got to think of much more exciting things to delight them.) I said, "I'm sorry, Ben. I can't take you with me this time because you touched something last time. I want you to stay home with Mom and think about that."

Crying, Ben stayed home with Carrie. The girls jumped into the car, and off we went. We talked about the No Touch rule on the way there and on the way home. It was a successful experience, and I let them know that I was pleased.

A while later, I made yet another trip. This time, Ben went with us and enjoyed a successful time. I was teaching my children a new rule, but more importantly, the rule was teaching them a new value—self-discipline.

After about six months of practicing the No Touch rule in the video store, grocery store, bank, and neighbors' houses, the children understood. They had developed enough self-discipline that when I took them into a gift shop, they wouldn't touch anything. In fact, Carrie and I soon began receiving compliments on how well behaved our children were. Occasionally, they would make a mistake, and we would quickly have them sit down right where they were and think about the No Touch rule.

All was going well until the Saturday I took the kids with me to a repair store to get the lawnmower fixed. I remember that day well. My three younger children weren't touching a thing, but they were jumping around, playing tag, and just being rambunctious while I talked to the salesman. When someone said, "Whose kids are these?" I felt like crawling into a hole. That's when I developed another self-discipline rule, the "Don't Be Wild" rule.

We still use this rule when we go into public places such as libraries, stores, museums, and church. It simply means that we carefully control ourselves in certain places so that we honor others.

Children can learn self-discipline at home through a number of rules. Bedtimes teach children that they go to bed on schedule even if they're not tired. Practicing the piano, cleaning up their rooms, and getting homework done each day all teach children self-discipline.

Personal Boundaries

Establishing a "Stop" rule is also important because it can help reduce much of the bickering between siblings. Teasing or tickling isn't always wrong and, in fact, can add an element of playfulness to family dynamics. But during a teasing or tickling game, usually one person wants to be done before the other is ready to quit. This dynamic sets people up for frustration, anger, and tears.

The Stop rule teaches children the value of their words. When any child wants to end a teasing or tickling game, he or she can say stop, and the other person must stop immediately. This rule allows children to set limits on others' behavior toward them. It allows any child, young or old, to set a boundary and know when that boundary is violated. This levels the playing field among siblings, so all family members can feel safe, knowing that they can use their words to protect themselves. Even when Dad tickles his daughter, she should be able to say stop, and Dad should stop.

Remember, though, that boundaries such as the Stop rule are not useful unless there's a place to appeal. Children who believe that other people have violated their boundaries must have somewhere to turn. So it's important for you to be available to help children use the Stop rule appropriately and back up the words if the other person doesn't stop.

Sometimes, children selfishly try to misuse this boundary idea. They ask for a game to stop temporarily so that they can get the upper hand and then restart the game. A child may say stop, then turn around and tease back. This can add an element of confusion to the Stop rule. Encourage children to use such words as "Time" or "I'm on base" for temporary pauses and to use the Stop rule only for ending the game.

At first, parents are often skeptical of this rule. One mom admitted, "I remember thinking, *Yeah right! No way is this going to work with my kids.* But one day I was so desperate that I tried it. I explained the Stop rule to my kids—and it worked! I was amazed. I even used it when I went on vacation with my sister. Her kids were driving me crazy with all their teasing, so I taught *them* the Stop rule, too. It worked again!"

Helping children to set up boundaries teaches them to establish limits in other areas of their lives, too. When kids learn to recognize boundaries, defend them, and receive help from responsible adults, they are less likely to become silent victims of abuse. Sometimes, children are mistreated physically or sexually and then plagued with guilt and self-condemnation. They are caught in a bind because although they know they've been mistreated, they also hesitate to speak out against the offender. Abuse and its solutions are complicated, but at least part of the solution is teaching children how to defend personal boundaries.

WHEN KIDS LEARN TO RECOGNIZE BOUNDARIES, DEFEND THEM, AND RECEIVE HELP FROM RESPONSIBLE ADULTS, THEY ARE LESS LIKELY TO BECOME SILENT VICTIMS OF ABUSE.

Establish Rules with Teens

It's no secret that rules usually cause problems for teenagers. They think differently than they did when they were young. They're away from home more, often in new situations, and must make decisions that are more complex than just abiding by certain rules. If all they know is a list of rules, they may have a hard time knowing what to do in a new environment offering many choices. Furthermore, adolescents are in the midst of a God-given process of developing their value systems. If parents only spend time creating rules, they're expecting their young people to translate those rules into everyday life and decide what's really important all by themselves. This is often unreasonable and why teaching values is vital. Children of all ages can learn how to apply rules in different ways when faced with new situations if they have at least some understanding of the values behind the rules.

Perhaps you have a teenager who disagrees with your convictions or doesn't apply them to life the same way you do. Your rules will help to clarify your expectations and allow family life to run more smoothly. They also serve as markers for a young person who is trying to develop a value system for life. Remember, rules change, but values remain the same.

As children grow up, they often pressure parents to drop rules they think they've outgrown. Parents are sometimes reluctant to do that because they know that certain rules serve important purposes in teenagers' lives. For example, a young man named Tom said to his parents, "We shouldn't have a rule that says I have to clean my room before I spend time with my friends on Saturday. I'm fourteen years old."

He and his parents reevaluated that rule. Since Tom was generally neat and took care of his things, they decided to remove that rule for a time to see if Tom could do well. As it turned out, he did just fine, and they didn't have to reinstate the rule.

When Tom's brother, Mike, turned fourteen, he said to his parents, "You stopped the rule about cleaning our rooms when Tom was fourteen. I think I shouldn't have that rule now, either." Mike's parents reevaluated the rule, but this time they decided that it was helpful because Mike tended to become more and more messy unless an outward guideline pressured him.

As we've seen, rules provide guidelines and clarify expectations for parents and children. Sara's son, Jeremy, just turned thirteen. She often agreed to her son's requests without fully realizing what she was getting herself into. "I feel like I'm a taxicab driver," she said, "shuttling children to friends' homes, sports events, music lessons, and church activities. I don't mind taking my son places because of the benefits of those activities, but I don't like the surprise of finding out that I'm the chaperone or that I'm responsible for picking up other children or going to get my son at some late hour of the night.

"To address this problem, I developed a 'Complete Proposal' rule. My son has to bring a complete proposal to me when asking permission for activities. We've posted the following questions on our bulletin board, and he knows that they all must be answered before I give permission.

- ☐ What do you want to do?
- ☐ Where will it take place?
- ☐ Who's in charge?
- ☐ Who's driving?
- ☐ When do you need to be there?
- ☐ When and how will you return home?
- ☐ How much will it cost?
- ☐ How will you accomplish your other responsibilities while you are gone?"

Not only did Sara recognize a problem in family life and add a new rule to solve it, she helped her son understand the value behind it. The Complete Proposal rule helped

Jeremy develop thoroughness in his decision making. As he thought through the answers to the questions, he sometimes even changed his mind, recognizing that an activity posed hidden challenges. This process also helped him to understand that differing expectations are a leading cause of conflict. By giving each other as much information as possible, Sara and Jeremy worked to minimize misunderstandings and to prevent some of the anger that might otherwise have occurred.

When Parents Don't Agree on Rule Making

It's common for one parent to want to set different rules than the other. Although this can happen in any family, it's especially prevalent among single parents when a child spends part of the time with one parent and the rest of the time with the other. When parents disagree on the rules, it's usually because they're emphasizing different values. A more permissive parent may value relationship, while one who is stricter values a disciplined, structured lifestyle. Both values are important, but an overemphasis in one area often creates weaknesses in children. The closer the two parents can come in establishing common rules, the better, but cooperation between some parents seems elusive or even nonexistent.

If you are in this situation, do what you can to help the other parent understand your rules and why you think they're important. Be sure to emphasize the reasons behind your rules. You don't have to put down the other parent or react with anger. Just continue to hold the line with your rules and explain them often. As you discuss the underlying values, you may convince the other parent to see past the rules to the lessons your children need to learn.

Don't give up because the consistency between you and the other parent is lacking. When you've done all you can to move toward greater unity, remember the importance of your relationship with your children. You can have a significant effect on their development in the midst of the frustration. One parent who has strong convictions can have a tremendous impact on the lives of his or her children.

As you share your convictions with them, you are teaching the values behind the rules. When your children grow up, they will have to decide for themselves which rules they will choose. By explaining yourself well and emphasizing the values behind the rules, you'll prepare your children to make wise decisions when they get older.

As we (Scott and Joanne) work with families on an individual basis, we often help confused children caught in the midst of the single-parent dilemma. Among other things, we discuss rules and values with them.

Recently, we talked with Adrian. "You say that your dad requires that you make your bed, but your mom doesn't. It sounds like they run their families a little differently. When you get to be a mom someday, will you require that your children make their beds?"

This question helped us teach Adrian that her dad and mom have different values in family life and that she can learn good things from each of them. But someday she'll have to choose what she's going to do and what kind of rules she will establish for her family. Questions like these, and the ensuing discussions, help children process the multiple messages they receive.

It's Worth It!

Take the time to establish rules based on solid, biblical values. Your family will benefit because the underlying values will help your children grow and mature. In fact, many of the rules outlined in the Bible are helpful for family life. Children who learn these early will appreciate them even more as they get older.

Chapter 5

Dealing with Anger in Children

With the instruction booklet in one hand and a lighter in the other, Craig twisted the knob of the small burner on the camping stove. His family had been looking forward to this trip for weeks, but he had forgotten how much work setting up camp could be. *I'm glad we're here with some other families. That will add to the fun.* Craig paused to watch his son play with two young friends on the edge of the woods.

As he looked up—ouch!—a small rock hit Aaron, age ten, in the leg. Aaron picked up a piece of the gravel and threw it back, jumping behind a tree. Aaron's father, Brad, was in the next campsite. He had paused from pounding in a tent peg to watch the boys.

"Aaron, come over here please," Brad called. "I'd like to talk to you."

Aaron came running over, and Brad bent down to have a quiet discussion with his son.

Craig kept one eye on the interaction as he fiddled some more with the knob. He smiled as the burner came to life.

After a few seconds, Aaron ran back to his friends. "Guys, we can't throw rocks anymore. Let's go collect some sticks for roasting marshmallows."

Wow! That went pretty well. No fuss. No fights. I wonder how he did that? Craig had observed Brad, Annette, and their kids for the past several hours. He had noticed that the Wilson kids responded to their parents' discipline without arguing or defensiveness. *Why didn't Aaron get angry when he was corrected?* Craig walked over to Brad's site. "Do your children always respond that way?"

Brad smiled. "What do you mean?"

"Aaron took it pretty well when you corrected him. How do you get him to accept your correction without getting upset or angry?"

Brad tied one end of a hammock to the tree between his site and Craig's. "Well, that's something we've been working on with him for years."

"My kids just aren't that sensitive. They don't seem to care that they've done the wrong thing. They get angry when I discipline them."

"Children have their own personalities, and some are more responsive than others. But we've worked hard to encourage sensitivity and openness with our kids."

"Yeah, that's it. There seems to be an openness in their relationship with you—even during discipline times."

Brad tied the other end of the hammock to another tree, carefully adjusting the tension. "One of the keys for us is that we don't discipline in anger. We try to respond to them with sorrow instead."

Craig's daughter, Jennifer, and her friends ran into camp. "Dad, could you play Frisbee with us?"

Craig motioned for her to wait while he finished talking with Brad. "Respond with sorrow? That's interesting. I'd like to hear more about that. Do you think Marlene and I could get together with you and Annette sometime and talk more?"

"Sure! Our kids are going fishing in about an hour with Ralph and Joey. We could get together then."

"Sounds good. Looks like it's playtime for me. See you soon."

Later, Craig and Marlene went over to visit with the Wilsons while Jennifer and Danny played at the campsite. After commenting on the great weather, Craig said, "Earlier you talked about the way you discipline your kids and how you choose sorrow over anger when you respond to their misbehavior. I find that my anger comes on without a choice."

Brad adjusted his chair. "Emotions are tricky. Lots of times people aren't aware of what's going on inside themselves. I used to get angry and then, after the fact, wonder what happened. Now, even when I'm angry, I'm more tuned in."

Marlene leaned forward. "But anger isn't always wrong. Even Jesus got angry. When Jennifer and Danny disobey or are mean to each other, that makes me mad."

Annette smiled. "Yes, anger comes pretty naturally to most of us. But anger is dangerous to relationships. It tends to put distance between people and makes them defensive."

Craig nodded. "That's a good point. So what did you do to get rid of anger in your family?"

Brad laughed. "Well, I wouldn't exactly say we've gotten rid of it, but we've developed a plan to deal with it."

"What kind of plan?" Marlene asked.

"Well, once Annette and I realized that anger was creating problems, we decided we needed to do something about it. We began talking with our children about anger, and we all agreed to work on it."

Annette continued. "We started by helping our children recognize when they were starting to get angry."

"Anger's pretty easy to see, isn't it?" Marlene asked.

"Sure, once it's full blown, but we wanted our kids to recognize their anger *before* they actually explode. So we observed each of our children and helped them to identify their warning signs that tell them—and us—that they're getting angry."

Craig laughed. "So you could get ready for the explosion?"

Brad smiled. "Well, actually, we realized they needed to stop and see the cues so they could deal with the anger before it got too intense."

"It would be hard for me to help our children deal with *their* anger when I'm having trouble controlling *mine*," Craig said.

"I can sure relate to that," Brad admitted. "It's a humbling thing to teach children about anger, because now they can recognize *my* anger more clearly. Working on this as a family has been a challenge, but we've all learned to apologize, forgive, and love each other more."

"You said that you respond with sorrow instead of anger," Craig said. "I'd like to hear more about that."

Brad turned to his wife. "Do you want to talk about that?"

Annette nodded. "Sure. We've found that sorrow opens relationships, while anger shuts things down. When we respond with anger, our kids become defensive. Sorrow is different. When we reflect sadness, dialogue opens up, and often the kids are motivated to change."

The conversation continued until the Wilson children returned from fishing. Craig and Marlene knew they were learning about another tool, something that would significantly change their family life. As they walked back to their campsite, Craig was already developing a plan. It wasn't long before he had the chance to test it.

"It's my flashlight!" Jennifer shouted from inside the tent.

"I just wanted to hold it. You don't have to grab!" Danny yelled.

Craig opened the tent flap and leaned inside. "What's going on in here?"

"He—"

"Danny, I want you to come out of the tent and leave the flashlight here."

"But I was just looking at it."

"Come on, Danny. Obey me and come out."

Danny climbed out of the tent.

"Jennifer," Craig said slowly, "it makes me sad when you don't share with your brother. That doesn't seem loving." Craig watched to see Jennifer's response.

Jennifer crossed her arms and pouted. "Yeah, but he'll just break it."

Craig continued softly. "Danny doesn't have a flashlight. I wish you would allow him to use it instead of just demanding that he return it."

Jennifer uncrossed her arms but continued to look away from her dad.

Craig didn't know what else to say, so he walked away, leaving Jennifer in the tent. *She's developed some pretty tough patterns of defensiveness. I'm not sure this will work. She certainly didn't change her attitude this time.*

Craig began to stack firewood. About ten minutes later, he heard Jennifer and Danny talking.

"You can use it as long as you're careful," Jennifer said.

"Okay, I'll be careful."

Craig peeked in and saw Jennifer hand Danny the flashlight. *It worked! By responding with gentleness and sorrow, I think I encouraged a more compassionate side in her.* "That's nice, Jennifer. I like the way you're showing love to your brother."

Jennifer smiled at her dad.

Thank you, Lord, Craig prayed as he walked toward the picnic table.

USING TOOL 5: A PLAN FOR ANGER KEEPS RELATIONSHIPS OPEN

Most families don't have a plan for dealing with anger. They just continue on, hoping things will get better. When families don't resolve their anger, however, they just keep trying to start over. Trying again is helpful, but we each need to have a bigger plan if we want negative patterns of anger to change.

Taking Anger Seriously

One day, a man arrived home from work at five o'clock, as usual. He quickly discovered that his wife had not had a good day. As a result, she had a short fuse and an unpleasant attitude. Nothing he said or did was right. By seven, things had not improved, so he said, "Why don't I go outside, pretend that I've just arrived home, come back in, and start all over."

His wife agreed.

He went outside, came back in, and announced in a loving voice, "Honey, I'm home!"

"And just where have you been?" she replied sharply. "It's seven o'clock!"

ANGER ISN'T ALWAYS WRONG, BUT IT IS ALWAYS DANGEROUS.

This simple illustration reveals a key point: dealing with anger appropriately requires more than just starting over. We parents need to understand anger and develop a strategy for working on it in family life. Some of us, afraid of anger in our children, walk around in fear that we'll trip a wire that sets off an emotional explosion. This response to anger is never helpful. In order to avoid responding in fear, let's explore how to deal with anger constructively. After all, we have the privilege and responsibility of guiding changes that must take place within our families.

Anger Isn't Always Wrong

Before we actually get into specifics concerning anger management, we need to recognize this: *anger isn't always wrong, but it's always dangerous.* Anger is like a warning light on a dashboard. It flashes to indicate that something is possibly, though not certainly, wrong. For example, the following verses warn about anger but don't prohibit it altogether:

◻ "'In your anger do not sin': Do not let the sun go down while you are still angry" (Eph. 4:26).

◻ "Everyone should be quick to listen, slow to speak and slow to become angry" (James 1:19).

The Bible also tells us that Jesus became angry. In Mark 3:3–5, we learn significant lessons about how we should control our anger:

> Jesus said to the man with the shriveled hand, "Stand up in front of everyone."
>
> Then Jesus asked them [the Pharisees], "Which is lawful on the Sabbath: to do good or to do evil, to save life or to kill?" But they remained silent.
>
> He looked around at them in anger and, deeply distressed at their stubborn hearts, said to the man, "Stretch out your hand." He stretched it out, and his hand was completely restored.

Jesus became angry for a good reason. He saw the Pharisees' stubborn hearts. But instead of reacting in anger, he did something constructive. He healed the man.

Anger isn't necessarily wrong, but it is dangerous if not guided appropriately. That's why Ephesians 4:31 reads, "Get rid of all bitterness, rage and anger, brawling and slander, along with every form of malice." Six kinds of anger are mentioned in this verse. We'll explore the first three—bitterness, rage, and anger—later in this chapter. (We won't go into detail on the last three, but let us quickly define them. What is *brawling*? If you have more than one child, you know that brawling is fighting because someone is angry. *Slander* is talking evil about someone because of anger, and *malice* is planning evil against another person because of anger.)

Benefits of an Anger-management Plan

Anger is like a virus. It's contagious. It's crippling. It decreases productivity and peace. It decreases our ability to enjoy life. But there is a treatment, and the younger the patient, the easier the cure. If you can help yourself and your family understand the anger you all experience, and make adjustments, you can live more peaceful lives. Unfortunately, most families don't deal with anger directly.

AS YOU IMPLEMENT A PLAN FOR ANGER MANAGEMENT IN YOUR FAMILY, RELATIONSHIPS WILL OPEN UP, INDIVIDUALS WILL GROW CLOSER TOGETHER, AND YOUR CHILDREN WILL LEARN AND APPLY CONSTRUCTIVE COMMUNICATION SKILLS.

Are you willing to partner with your family to work on a preventative anger-management plan? If so, your humility and teachable spirit will show a lot to your children and your spouse if you are married. They will see spiritual growth that brings about godly character in you.

Growth in anger management doesn't happen overnight, but by using the tools of time, consistent work, prayer, and self-awareness, your family can get anger under control. As you implement a plan for anger management in your family, relationships will open up, individuals will grow closer together, and your children will learn and apply constructive communication skills. You'll also learn to deal with conflict in healthy ways and have a more peaceful family life.

Eventually, you will be able to recognize your own developing anger and choose more appropriate responses and courses of action. You'll be able to handle anger in positive ways. In short, you'll all receive a valuable gift.

Anger can be divided into four categories: frustration, anger, rage, and bitterness. These words describe what people experience as the irritation they feel continues unchecked. To effectively address anger, you need a plan to deal with it in all four areas. We can illustrate graduated intensity of angry feelings using a picture of a thermometer. The feeling often starts with frustration and builds to anger, rage, and finally bitterness.

Five Steps Toward an Anger-management Plan

There are five essential steps in helping children deal positively with their anger. We'll explore each one.

Step 1: Identify Cues That Indicate Your Children Are Getting Angry

The Bible tells us to be "slow to become angry" (James 1:19). But many children move quickly from a trigger to an angry reaction. A trigger might be an unkind comment from a sibling, a request to do a chore, or a difficult part of a homework assignment. The best way to slow down this reaction is to identify early warning signs that indicate anger is approaching. Children often don't recognize anger. In fact, many times they act out before they even realize what happened. This first step helps children become more aware of their feelings and better able to control them.

Before you help your children recognize the cues earlier,
think about the cues that tell you when you're starting to get
angry. One dad said, "My eyebrows turn down, and my fore-
head becomes tense. My shoulders raise, and I tend to lean
forward. My voice becomes louder and more strained."

How can you tell when you're getting frustrated? Here are
common cues in children that indicate they're starting to get
angry:

- They tense up and clench their teeth.
- Their behavior increases in intensity.
- They begin to cry or feel like crying.
- Their tone changes to whining or sarcasm.
- They become restless, withdrawn, unresponsive, or eas-
  ily provoked.
- They begin to talk incessantly, often with greater
  intensity.
- They make noises like growls or deep breathing.
- They pout.
- They squint, roll their eyes, or develop other facial
  expressions.

Take time to jot down the cues that each of your children
demonstrates when get-
ting angry. Once you've
identified these cues,
teach your children how
to recognize them. Your
job is to help your chil-
dren recognize their feelings of anger and identify
specific positive actions to
take before the anger
becomes more intense.

**HELP YOUR CHILDREN RECOGNIZE
THEIR FEELINGS OF ANGER AND
IDENTIFY SPECIFIC POSITIVE
ACTIONS TO TAKE BEFORE THE
ANGER BECOMES MORE INTENSE.**

For very young children, you can point out that this emotion is called anger and offer suggestions for responding differently. For older kids, you might walk them through the four phases of anger, telling them why it's important to gain control before they move past frustration.

Let's say, for example, that a dad sees frustration (an early type of anger) developing in his son, who can't get his sneakers on. "I can tell you're getting angry," Dad might say, "because your voice is getting louder and you're squinting your eyes." The boy needs to recognize his frustration before he becomes so angry that he throws the sneaker across the room.

If your teenage daughter is frustrated because the shirt she wants to wear is in the laundry or is wrinkled, you can help her recognize that frustration and deal with it appropriately before it intensifies into anger or rage.

> **THE PRINCIPLE YOU TEACH THROUGH WORDS AND PARENTAL CONTROL IS THAT "ANGRY PEOPLE ARE UNHAPPY PEOPLE."**

In this step of identifying the cues, you can use various methods to raise anger awareness. One fun way is to ask your children how they can tell when *you* are starting to get angry. Children seem to come up with answers quickly: "Your eyes get bigger" or "You raise your voice." Children benefit from recognizing the anger cues of other people because it helps them to become more sensitive to their own physical signs. (If you use this method, be sure to respond honestly, and don't give excuses for your inappropriate anger.)

Another way you might help your kids learn about anger is to watch a children's video with them. Most animated movies contain lots of emotion, and nonverbal cues are exaggerated. Have a child stop the video when he or she sees anger in one of the characters. Then ask, "How can you tell that person is angry?" Children often learn to see anger in others first before they can identify it in themselves.

Important note: If your children aren't ready to work on anger, you won't get very far. Before you use an anger-management plan, you may need to whet their appetites a bit. This usually comes in the form of more consequences, tighter restrictions, and greater firmness. The principle you teach through words and parental control is that "angry people are unhappy people." Eventually, your children will learn that their anger is their problem and that if they want to be happy, they had better do something about it instead of ignoring it or blaming their anger on others—or on life.

Step 2: Step Back When Anger Starts

One of the healthiest ways to respond to anger at any of its stages is to "step back." This gives children (and parents) time to acknowledge that anger is developing, to rethink the situation, calm down, and determine what to do next. Otherwise, frustrations can easily build, rage can become destructive, and bitterness can form. Stepping back helps to stop the progression of intensity and gives children time to respond differently.

Unfortunately, many children (and adults) don't want to step back when they're angry. Instead, they want to press forward and even attack. The anger they feel is so intense that they need to make heart-level changes before they can respond with constructive behavior.

When children lack the self-control to work on anger, they need parental control to help them. Let's say that you tell your child to take a Break, but your child begins to badger, argue, and push your buttons. And even when you attempt to leave the situation, your child follows you, continuing to press with intensity. This manipulative technique is designed to draw you into a fight. Don't engage! Determine not to allow the child to bait you into an argument. If you start fighting back, he or she will escape the important lessons of anger management and learn to use anger to control other people— including you! Have the child sit in the hall or on the stairs to settle down. Children must learn this step in order to respond well to anger, and it may require your firmness to teach it. Whether you stand there or leave, make it clear that you're done with the conversation until your child takes a Break.

> **WHEN YOU TEACH YOUR CHILDREN TO STEP BACK AND EVALUATE THE SITUATION, YOU ARE TEACHING THEM WISDOM AND MATURITY.**

Children learn that stepping back may just involve looking away or taking a deep breath. Other times, it may mean changing the activity or walking away. During the most intense moments, it may mean leaving the situation or getting alone. The child who is frustrated with a puzzle, for example, may choose to work on something else for a while. The girl who is angry with her brother may need to cool off in another room.

When you teach your children to step back and evaluate the situation, you are teaching them wisdom and maturity. After all, this is a skill many adults do not possess. Many moms and dads would benefit from stepping back when anger starts to take over.

Another activity that's helpful when teaching children about anger is the "stop-sign journal." Draw three stop signs, increasing in size, and leave room to write underneath each one. Ask your children to give examples of frustration, anger, and rage. Then write those under the small, medium, and large stop signs, respectively. Finally, ask your children to suggest how a person might stop or step back in each situation.

Step 3: Choose a Better Response Than Anger

Many parents move to choosing better responses too quickly, thinking that the complete solution lies here. Although this step is important, it won't work alone. The first two steps are essential. In fact, just doing the first two steps will go a long way in helping your children to learn anger control. Only then are they ready for this step.

While children step back, they can choose more appropriate responses to their situations. As children see the effect their anger has on others, they begin to see the need to control themselves. They need to learn that they can control their anger and that the way they respond is their choice. If you tell Susie to go to bed and she gets angry, the way she responds is up to her. She can stomp off and slam the door; or she can choose to adjust her expectations, accept your instruction, and remain calm.

STATEMENTS SUCH AS "QUIT POUTING" OR "STOP HITTING" DON'T PROVIDE ENOUGH INFORMATION FOR CHILDREN TO KNOW WHAT THEY SHOULD DO INSTEAD.

People who always blame others view themselves as victims. Children need to take responsibility for their actions, even when they're responding out of emotion. They must not blame their hurtful responses on someone else. (And, of course, parents must not blame their anger on other people, either. A child's wrong behavior doesn't give a parent the right to use anger as a weapon.) Parents and children both need to take responsibility for themselves. They need to learn to control their anger and choose to respond in appropriate ways.

But what better choices should children make? Parents who are frustrated about their kids' anger often respond negatively, pointing out the wrongs without suggesting alternatives. Statements such as "Quit pouting" or "Stop hitting" don't provide enough information for children to know what they should do instead.

Parents need to teach their children other alternatives, and simplifying the choices makes the decision process easier. Here are three positive healthy choices to get kids started:

- ☐ *Talk about it.* If six-year-old Carl doesn't like the way Trevor is playing with his favorite car, he can recognize the anger (frustration) and choose to talk about it by saying, "I don't like it when you play rough with my car." Talking about it can help solve the problem without saying or doing something hurtful.

- ☐ *Get help.* A second choice Carl has is to get help. A third party can give counsel and advice and help resolve the situation without anger. This may be another child, a parent, or a teacher.

- ☐ *Slow down and persevere.* Sometimes children who are becoming angry can choose a third option: to take a deep breath and determine to persevere. Just acknowledging his frustration may allow Carl to continue to play with Trevor without becoming angry. You might explain perseverance to a child this way: "If you're cleaning out your closet and the bucket of Legos suddenly falls off a shelf, instead of kicking your blocks across your room in anger, you can slow down and persevere. That means that you stop for a moment, go back to the problem, and pick up the blocks. This approach will help you get through the problem without making it worse."

You can help your children learn to handle their anger by reflecting what you see and offering assistance without telling them what to do. "Jeremy, I can tell you're getting angry because your voice is getting louder. Remember you have three other alternatives. If you need help, just ask me." Even though it may be easy to get caught up in your children's emotions and try to solve problems for them, don't do it. It's better to help them process their emotions rather than solve the problems.

Step 4: Control Rage; Don't Vent It

When children's anger progresses beyond frustration and controlled anger, they become enraged. Rage is anger out of control. Enraged children no longer think rationally. Their anger is now controlling them. You may see a host of venting behaviors such as yelling, hitting, saying mean things, kicking, screaming, manipulative behaviors, and/or withdrawal. When a young child is enraged, we call it a "tantrum." But rage isn't reserved for young children. Even some adults have a problem with rage; we just don't call it a tantrum.

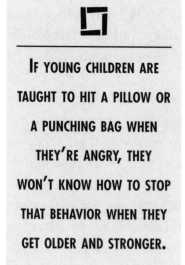

IF YOUNG CHILDREN ARE TAUGHT TO HIT A PILLOW OR A PUNCHING BAG WHEN THEY'RE ANGRY, THEY WON'T KNOW HOW TO STOP THAT BEHAVIOR WHEN THEY GET OLDER AND STRONGER.

Whatever form it takes, children (and adults) must learn to control rage and not vent it. Proverbs 29:11 reads, "A fool gives full vent to his anger, but a wise man keeps himself under control." Allowing children to vent anger is dangerous for them and anyone else around. If young children are taught to hit a pillow or a punching bag when they're angry, they won't know how to stop that behavior when they get older and stronger.

One boy was allowed to kick the furniture when he became angry. His mom called it "letting off steam." When he grew up, he still kicked the furniture—plus his car, his dog, and anything else that got in his way, including his wife and kids. No. It's not okay. Venting anger teaches children an unhealthy response pattern. Children must learn anger control and rage reduction early in life, so they have the opportunity to develop habits of self-control and healthy communication.

After a temper tantrum is over, require a discussion. Use the Positive Conclusion mentioned in chapter 2 as a guide. As you and your child reflect on what went wrong, talk about inappropriate ways to handle anger. Be sure to validate the angry feelings when appropriate, and distinguish between the emotion and the child's response. "I understand that you're angry because Joe took your CD without asking. That makes sense, but we have to solve the problem differently because hitting him is wrong." Talk about a better way to respond next time. This kind of discussion after each episode can help a child learn to rethink anger and build new positive patterns.

Keep in mind that your goal of anger control may take some time. You're trying to decrease the frequency and the intensity of angry episodes. *Frequency* has to do with the number of times a child loses his temper. *Intensity* has to do with the amount of anger the child pours into the situation. Reducing both is important. Talk to your children about this goal, and point out examples of the improvements you're seeing. "Bobby, I know you got angry with Josh a few minutes ago, but it seems that you stopped from becoming too intense. I like that." Or, "Shannon, you used to get angry a lot, but it seems that more recently you're not getting angry as often. Good job."

Step 5: Choose Forgiveness, Not Bitterness

Anger has many faces, and bitterness is one of the ugliest. *Bitterness* is anger connected to hurt from the past, the ability to catalog painful memories so they can be used at any time to fuel present anger. Bitterness harbors anger for longer periods of time than other forms of anger. Some people don't think of themselves as angry because they don't experience rage. Instead, their frustration and anger go straight to bitterness. Bitterness is much easier to deal with in children than in adults, but it's dangerous nonetheless.

Children may be experiencing bitterness if they are

- using such phrases as "You always ... !" or "You never ... !";
- responding in anger more frequently and intensely than the situations warrant;
- using sarcasm or becoming cynical;
- becoming negative and critical; or
- withdrawing and becoming unresponsive.

These symptoms don't always mean that a child is bitter, but they may indicate a problem. Bitter and resentful children need to see what their anger is doing to them. Holding on to offenses as a type of revenge is not helpful. People were not created to carry around thoughts and plans of revenge. They need to let it go. When children hold on to offenses, they become miserable, plotting revenge, developing a critical spirit, and are generally unhappy.

Don't ignore bitterness. Don't assume that children will outgrow it. If anger isn't dealt with, it gets worse. Address it. Talk about it. It may mean listening to your children and communicating understanding. Resentful children sometimes feel as if they're misunderstood and that no one listens to them.

You might say, "It sounds like you're still angry about not being able to go to your friend's house yesterday."

Children need a plan for dealing with ongoing offenses such as meanness, unfairness, and rejection. Confrontation can bring resolution to a problem, but justice isn't always possible. Bitterness is a poor choice for coping with the unfairness of life because it turns the offended person into an angry person.

The solution to bitterness is forgiveness.

Forgiveness, a heart-level response that can ease anger, is not about forgetting an offense. Children sometimes hesitate to forgive because they think they must forget that an offense occurred or ignore the pain it caused. Forgiveness acknowledges the offense and chooses to let go of the desire for revenge, recognizing that God is the Judge. (See Rom. 12:18–19.) Forgiveness means letting go and moving on, not holding the offense against someone any longer. Forgiveness is a mature and healthy response that says, in effect, "You have done wrong to me, but I am responsible for my own actions and my response to you. I choose to let go of the offense."

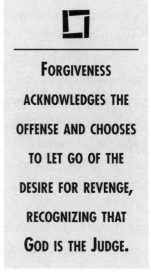

FORGIVENESS ACKNOWLEDGES THE OFFENSE AND CHOOSES TO LET GO OF THE DESIRE FOR REVENGE, RECOGNIZING THAT GOD IS THE JUDGE.

Once children understand forgiveness, healthy confrontation can take place. Children need to learn about forgiveness and understand how to clean out their anger tank every day. Ephesians 4:26 reads, "Do not let the sun go down while you are still angry." A good anger-management plan contains a strategy for dealing with accumulated anger and preventing it from hampering one's life.

Long-term Anger Management: What You Can Do

In order to help children deal with their anger, you need a plan that addresses more than just explosions. Here are some other suggestions to help you address the anger in your kids.

First, take an internal look to see if an anger problem is in your heart. Maybe your expectations are unrealistic, or a demanding attitude is getting in the way. Sometimes we as parents become angry with our kids because we believe they've violated our rights, such as the right to peace and quiet or the right to a neat house. Our anger often provokes anger in our children.

If you are angry, take responsibility for it. With practice and a huge dose of God's grace, you can change your patterns and responses. The warning light on the dashboard doesn't have to stay on or be set to light up when the least irritation arises.

Help your children to develop positive character qualities in order to alleviate some of their anger. Some anger problems occur in children because their character isn't developed to the point where they are able to manage their intense feelings. Teaching children to be kind, compassionate, humble, gentle, patient, and forgiving will help to reduce anger. As children develop godly character, they will experience fewer problems with emotions being out of control. Qualities like patience and tolerance help children to turn obstacles into opportunities instead of frustrations. Patience is waiting for something with a sense of contentment. Tolerance is putting up with an irritation without allowing it to provoke anger.

Help reduce anger in your children by filling their emotional tanks. Anger is emotionally draining. Furthermore, when emotional tanks are nearing empty, anger more easily accelerates from frustration to controlled anger, to rage, and finally to bitterness. Hug, touch, and encourage your children on a consistent and frequent basis. They need individual, loving attention each day. Talk with them; listen to them; make eye contact with them. Let them know they are valuable and important to you. Children with full emotional tanks can tolerate much more than children whose tanks are almost empty.

Identify ways that you may be contributing to an anger problem. Parents can exasperate or embitter their children. (See Eph. 6:4; Col. 3:21.) Your mistakes don't justify your children's anger, but if you need to make changes, it's best to acknowledge this and begin making the appropriate adjustments. Proverbs 15:1 reads, "A gentle answer turns away wrath, but a harsh word stirs up anger." Your harshness can heighten a child's anger problem.

Watch out for unrealistic expectations for your children. Such expectations can cause anger in kids, who begin to feel helpless, hopeless, or out of control. Sometimes you may need to just step back and ask yourself, *Am I expecting too much?* Unrealistic expectations can be a primary cause of bitterness.

Model appropriate responses to anger. Children sometimes think that they are the only ones who experience frustration. Being more transparent about your feelings will help your children deal with theirs. You may say, "Boy, I'm frustrated; I can't find my keys." Or, "I need to be alone for a few minutes to settle down; let's talk about this some more later."

Remember, your gentleness will go a lot further than expressing anger. Try it. It works. Children often respond to gentleness when they're upset. In the introductory story, Craig responded to Jennifer with sorrow instead of anger when she was unwilling to share her flashlight. Thus he invited communication and open relationship. Sorrow is a much more "relationship friendly" response than anger.

It's Worth It!

If your family struggles with anger management, putting into practice the techniques we've explored here will teach children solutions they'll use for the rest of their lives. Work on anger as a family. It may take some time, but your children will learn valuable lessons in family life about emotions and how to deal with them.

Here's a quick summary of how to develop a family anger-management plan.

1. Identify cues that indicate your children are getting angry.
2. Step back when anger starts.
3. Choose a better response than anger.
4. Control rage; don't vent it.
5. Choose forgiveness, not bitterness.

Chapter 6

Disciplining Consistently Even When You're Tired

Marlene took a sip of tea and settled on the couch with her book. Just as she turned the first page, she heard feet shuffling in the hallway. Her eye caught Danny peeking around the corner. Glancing at her watch, she sighed. "It's 8:30. Get back into bed, Danny."

"I want a drink of water."

"Get a drink; then get right back into bed."

On his way back from the kitchen, Danny paused in the doorway. "What are you doing?"

"I'm reading. You need to go to bed."

Danny fidgeted. "I'm not tired."

"Look, you're going to be tired if you don't go to bed. Besides, you have to get up early."

"But I can't sleep."

Marlene was too tired to fight. "All right. You can sit with me for a few minutes. Then you're going back to bed, okay?"

"Okay." Danny smiled and jumped up on the couch.

Marlene didn't really want Danny to stay up, but she didn't have the energy to put him into bed again. It seemed as though this happened every night. Last night she had to lie down with him to get him to stay in bed, but then she ended up falling asleep.

I wish four-year-olds could go to bed by themselves.

"Hi, honey," Craig called as he entered the front door.

Marlene looked up. "Thanks for getting the milk."

"Hi, Daddy."

Craig frowned at Danny. "What are you doing up? I said good night to you before I left."

"I'm not tired."

"Well, it's late. You need to be in bed."

"Your dad's right. Get into bed. You had a busy day today, and tomorrow's a school day."

"But, Mom, you said I could sit here with you."

Craig took the milk into the kitchen, then returned. "No," he said, "you need to go to bed now, Danny. Come on. I'll help you get there."

Marlene sighed. "Thanks, Craig."

Craig returned as Marlene put away the milk. "It's pretty late for Danny to be up."

"I know. I put him to bed at 7:30, but he kept getting up. I didn't want to fight about it. I just wanted to relax a little before Mom stops by."

"Your mother's coming over?"

"She has some clothes for the kids." Marlene glanced at the clock. "She'll be here any minute."

Marlene's mother, Karen, lived nearby and often helped out with the kids. Marlene enjoyed their relationship and benefited from her mother's support and encouragement.

"Mom?" Danny called from the bedroom.

Marlene rolled her eyes and turned toward the bedroom just as her mother appeared at the front door.

"Come on in, Mom. I'll be right back."

Marlene told Danny to stop calling and go to sleep. Then she joined her mother and Craig in the kitchen.

Karen pulled a shirt out of a bag and held it up. "Kelly from work gave me these clothes, and I thought they might fit Jennifer."

"Thanks," Marlene said. "Those things you brought for Danny were just the right size. I'll have Jennifer try these on tomorrow."

Karen sat down at the table. "Is Danny okay?"

"Oh, he's fine. He just had trouble going to bed tonight, as usual. He always seems to have an excuse to get up."

"You and your sisters used to try that, too, when you were little. The list of excuses can get pretty long: 'I need a drink'; 'I have to go to the bathroom'; 'I'm afraid of the dark'; 'I'm not tired yet'; 'I want a story'—or a kiss or a hug."

They all laughed.

"Come on, Mom. We didn't really do that when we were kids, did we?"

"At first you did, but we taught you to go to bed and stay there. All children go through these kinds of experiences, partly because they don't want to miss out on what Mom and Dad are doing."

"So what did you do?"

"Well, I think the secret is being consistent."

"Oh, Mom. Every parenting book we read talks about being consistent. It would be nice if one would tell us how, especially when I'm tired and have other things to do in life besides putting Danny back in bed."

"You're right. It is hard. Parenting is a never-ending job. I remember times I was just dead tired. It's difficult to be consistent when you'd like to take the evening off."

Marlene sighed. "I'd like to be off duty once I say good night."

Her mother smiled and thought for a moment. "As I look back on it now, I see things from a different perspective. The job of parenting is so important. Each problem you face now is an opportunity to help Jennifer and Danny learn and grow."

"It's sure easy to lose that perspective in the midst of the struggle," Craig added.

"I guess I should have been more firm tonight." Marlene crossed her arms and sat back in the chair. "But I just didn't feel like pushing it. It was easier to let him stay up a little longer."

Her mother moved the bag of clothes to the floor and leaned forward. "I understand, but in the long run I think you're making your job harder, and you're confusing Danny."

"What do you mean?"

"Well, sometimes you let him get up again, and sometimes you're firm about making him stay in bed. Danny must think it's always worth a try to get up, and then he probably wonders why sometimes it's not okay."

Karen paused and then continued. "If your discipline is based on your feelings or energy level, you end up being inconsistent. One time you feel ready to discipline; another time you don't."

"I know you're right, but how can anyone be consistent all the time? There are just too many battles to fight every day."

"That's true. You can't fight every battle, but you need to be consistent during the ones you do fight. One thing I've learned over the years is that consistent discipline has to be based on something more stable than how we feel."

"Like what?" Craig asked.

"I tried to focus on why I was disciplining. If I knew *why* I was doing what I was doing, it helped me to hang in there."

Marlene raised her eyebrows. "So you're saying I need to remember why my job is important."

"Yes, and it might be helpful to remember that training Jennifer and Danny now will have an impact for the rest of their lives. Being consistent will help Danny learn to stay in bed at night, but even more importantly, he'll develop self-discipline and self-control."

Craig thought for a moment. "Hmm, that's an interesting way to look at it."

Karen continued. "When I felt overwhelmed, I often reminded myself that God had given me this responsibility. Training you girls was my calling during that time of my life. Focusing on what's most important was a good motivation to press on when I felt like quitting."

Marlene looked at Craig. "I like this idea." Then she turned back to her mom. "What you're saying is ... if I had a clearer picture of why I discipline, it would be easier to choose my battles and be consistent."

"That was helpful for me, especially when I felt there was so much to do and so little energy left." Karen looked at the clock. "I've got to be going."

"This has been helpful." Craig stood up. "Thanks for stopping by."

"Thanks for the clothes," Marlene added, walking her mother to the door. "I know Jennifer will have fun trying them on."

The next evening, Marlene carried a cup of tea into the living room, where Craig was relaxing. "You know, as I worked with the kids today, I felt more motivated to discipline them."

"Really? Why was that?"

"Part of it was our conversation last night. It made me realize that the day-to-day discipline is important. I felt more motivated to follow through when I thought about my actions having lasting effects on the kids."

"Mom?" Danny appeared at the doorway.

"Danny, you're supposed to be in bed."

"I'm not tired. Can I sit here with you?"

Marlene looked at Craig, and they both smiled. "No way,

buddy." Marlene knew this was the beginning of the end of bedtime problems. It would take work, but she was ready for the challenge.

USING TOOL 6: A CLEAR PHILOSOPHY OF DISCIPLINE HELPS YOU PERSEVERE AND BE CONSISTENT

Inconsistent Discipline Results When Parents Feel Overwhelmed or Too Tired

When my (Joanne) son David was two, he loved to jump (disobediently) on the couch. I sometimes ignored this behavior because I was involved in my own activity and didn't want to take the time to deal with the problem. The irritation wasn't great enough to motivate me to take action. Can you relate?

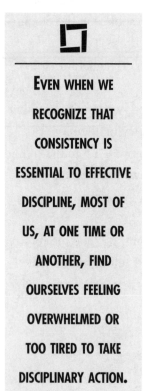

EVEN WHEN WE RECOGNIZE THAT CONSISTENCY IS ESSENTIAL TO EFFECTIVE DISCIPLINE, MOST OF US, AT ONE TIME OR ANOTHER, FIND OURSELVES FEELING OVERWHELMED OR TOO TIRED TO TAKE DISCIPLINARY ACTION.

Even when we recognize that consistency is essential to effective discipline, most of us, at one time or another, find ourselves feeling overwhelmed or too tired to take disciplinary action. We overlook our children's negative or unwanted behaviors until the irritation grows so much that we're compelled to do something. The result is inconsistent discipline, because what irritates us today may not seem irritating tomorrow.

In order to persevere and be consistent, we must develop a more solid motivation.

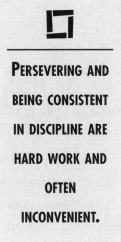

PERSEVERING AND BEING CONSISTENT IN DISCIPLINE ARE HARD WORK AND OFTEN INCONVENIENT.

As Craig and Marlene learned, we need something to hold on to when we're tired, discouraged, overwhelmed, or simply too busy dealing with the demands of life. Some of us burn out—even on a daily basis—because we don't know why we are parenting. Once we understand and apply a clear philosophy of discipline, however, we can reverse the trend of burnout and use it to strengthen our families. This philosophy will allow love, rather than anger, to be our motivation, and our children will know what to expect. Developing a clear philosophy of discipline can give us a foundation that will energize us when day-to-day problems seem overwhelming.

I (Joanne) used to be a runner. I would jog two to three times a week by a lake near our home. Running has many benefits, but there were days when I didn't feel like getting out there and running. Some days I had too much to do, I didn't have the energy, or the weather wasn't inviting. One day, I received an advertisement in the mail that read, "For most people, the hardest thing about exercise is ... sticking with it." The same thing could be said about parenting. Persevering and being consistent in discipline are hard work and often inconvenient.

Running and parenting have a number of similarities, and I've learned four success principles for running that apply to parenting. As you think about your job as a parent, imagine yourself being a runner. The four principles Scott and I will share in this chapter can keep us all "running" even when we feel like quitting. They can motivate us to take action when we feel too tired or preoccupied to discipline. These principles comprise what I call my philosophy of discipline. After you read mine, set aside time to think about and write down your own philosophy. Your principles may be the same as mine, or they may be different. Either way, you'll want to personalize them for your family.

Principle 1: Focus on the Goals

When I went running, I focused on a goal—to run around the lake two times (about two and a quarter miles). That's what I wanted to accomplish. I didn't chat with people I met or stop to fish in the lake. I was a runner with a goal.

You may develop a number of goals for your children over the years, but your children's primary job is to learn to obey and honor. Ephesians 6:1–3 reads, "Children, obey your parents in the Lord, for this is right. 'Honor your father and mother'—which is the first commandment with a promise— 'that it may go well with you and that you may enjoy long life on the earth.'"

There are many things that can sidetrack us, but teaching obedience and honor is to be the primary goal. Honoring and obeying don't come naturally; they need to be taught. We are the teachers. Each act of defiance or disobedience in our children is an important opportunity to teach these vital character qualities.

Your children will be blessed when they learn obedience and honor. Remembering this will give you clearer direction as you work with them. Stay focused on these goals, and you will discipline more consistently.

Obedience requires that a child give up his or her agenda for someone else in authority. It involves doing a task without being reminded and reporting back when that task is done. Children need to obey even when they think they have a better way, or they don't like what their parents are telling them. It's their responsibility to respond humbly, not to critique the parenting they receive. Learning this when children are young will help them become better students and, eventually, better employees.

Some children are strong willed, have their own agendas, and want others to follow their leadership. It's a challenge to raise a leader, but every good leader knows how to follow. Children need to learn to follow when they're young, or they will fail when they get older.

Certainly, children need to learn to take a stand for their convictions. Some parents hesitate to teach obedience for fear of squelching their children's initiative or independence. Children should primarily learn to stand for convictions with their peers and learn submission to authority from their parents.

Yes, evaluating authority can be helpful, but it's an advanced skill. There will come times when children critique authority-related requests and instructions. However, a prerequisite to taking a stand is a healthy sense of

> **WHEREAS OBEDIENCE GETS THINGS DONE, HONOR ADDRESSES HOW THOSE THINGS ARE DONE.**

submission and honor. Parents also need to lovingly teach their children how to obey so that these kids can, at some point, humbly express their convictions to those in authority.

Honor adds many more components. Honor treats people as special, does more than what's expected, and has a good attitude. Whereas obedience *gets* things done, honor addresses *how* those things are done.

I (Scott) was praising the obedience and responsiveness of my twelve-year-old son, Joshua. The friend with whom I was speaking said to Josh, "It sounds like you're going to grow up to be an old man."

Laughing, I turned to Josh and asked, "Do you know why he said that?"

"Yes," Josh replied. "It comes from that Bible verse that says if you honor your father and mother you will enjoy long life on the earth."

Principle 2: Endure the Pain

Running is hard work. It hurts. But successful runners persevere even though they experience resistance. Likewise, if you're going to be successful in discipline, be prepared for

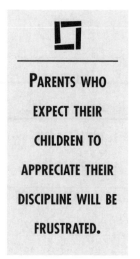

PARENTS WHO EXPECT THEIR CHILDREN TO APPRECIATE THEIR DISCIPLINE WILL BE FRUSTRATED.

resistance. Hebrews 12:11 reads, "No discipline seems pleasant at the time, but painful. Later on, however, it produces a harvest of righteousness and peace for those who have been trained by it."

Don't be surprised by resistance. That point seems obvious, but haven't you ever disciplined your child and then wondered if you did the right thing because he or she responded poorly? Do you second-guess yourself when your child responds negatively?

It's as if parents expect their children to say, "Thanks, Dad, for sending me to my room; I really appreciate the limits you set for me," or "I appreciate it, Mom, when you make me clean up my toys and make my bed." Children don't naturally respond this way. Parents who expect their children to appreciate their discipline will be frustrated.

When you send your son to his room, and he stomps all the way there and then slams the door, you now have two problems to deal with—the original offense and the bad attitude.

When your children resist discipline, it's important to look beyond the immediate struggle and focus on the future good. Remember, a child's immediate response is not an indicator of the discipline's effectiveness. Children don't naturally appreciate discipline and will usually respond negatively, at least when they are young.

You'll be motivated to persevere, however, if you remember that you are disciplining for greater long-term benefits such as building character in your children. Don't be surprised or discouraged by negative responses. Work to teach your kids to appreciate correction, but don't let their lack of responsiveness deter you from doing your job.

My calves hurt when I run, but that's no reason for me to give up. Children will respond negatively to discipline, but that's no reason to quit. Teaching children to respond to discipline appropriately takes time.

As your children grow wiser and you work with them to help them establish the right attitudes and condition of their hearts, they will learn to respond humbly and graciously to discipline and realize its value. The time you spend talking to your children about their attitudes will have lasting implications.

Here are some proverbs you can share with your kids that teach appropriate responses to discipline:

- "Whoever loves discipline loves knowledge, but he who hates correction is stupid" (Prov. 12:1).
- "A fool spurns his father's discipline, but whoever heeds correction shows prudence" (Prov. 15:5).
- "He who listens to a life-giving rebuke will be at home among the wise" (Prov. 15:31).

Principle 3: Look for Ways to Make It Positive

When I (Joanne) ran, I took my portable CD player with me and listened to praise music or books on tape. I looked for ways to make the experience more enjoyable, and this helped me to persevere.

Discipline works the same way. "Fathers," the apostle Paul wrote, "do not exasperate your children; instead, bring them up in the training and instruction of the Lord" (Eph. 6:4). The first part of this verse describes a negative way of relating to children. *Exasperate* gives the impression of being harsh and causing discouragement. In place of that negative response, fathers are instructed to do something positive, to bring their children up "in the training and instruction of the Lord." Discipline times are training times. They involve teaching. We should not discipline our children merely to get rid of negative behaviors. Our job is to train our children and show them the positive directions in which they are to go.

You may be thinking, *Yes, I know discipline is supposed to be positive, but how can I be positive when my kids are doing the wrong things?*

Perhaps you are tired and discouraged because you feel you're being too negative with your children. If so, it's time to break that cycle and focus on the positive.

Following are some proven tips to help you do this:

State rules and requests in positive terms whenever possible. Instead of saying, "Don't shout," you might say, "We need to talk quietly in this store." Clearly stating or restating a rule in positive terms gives your child a clear picture of what's expected and keeps your interaction on a positive note. This simple adjustment can help you as a parent focus on what you want your child to do instead of what you don't want.

Instead of complaining about the clothes scattered over your five-year-old daughter's room, you might say, "Remember, we put our dirty clothes in the hamper when we take them off." Give gentle, positive reminders to point the child in the right direction. Instead of saying, "Stop banging that drum," you might say, "You may play that drum outside or in your room." In this way, you are giving a choice of two positive options and focusing on a solution instead of complaining about a problem.

Look for approximately right behavior and affirm it. This will help to keep a positive atmosphere while disciplining. Don't wait until things are absolutely right. If you ask your child to clean up toys but find that only two of them are put away, you might say, "Oh, I see you put the blocks away. That's great! And I like the way you lined up your trucks. Now, I'd like you to put the balls in the box where they belong." In this way, you encourage steps in the right direction.

WHEN YOU INTERACT WITH YOUR CHILDREN ABOUT THINGS THEY'RE DOING RIGHT, YOU MAKE DISCIPLINE A POSITIVE EXPERIENCE.

When you interact with your children about things they're doing right, you make discipline a positive experience. You will feel encouraged and motivated to continue on to be the effective parent God wants you to be.

Let's say that your teenage son tries to make a meal for the family but doesn't get it quite right. Praise him for his initiative and hard work. Teens make mistakes, but often hidden within those mistakes are good qualities needing guidance. Encourage children for their desire to try, especially when a sense of failure might otherwise loom on the horizon.

When my (Joanne) son Timothy was learning to dress himself, we had a rule that he needed to be dressed before coming to the breakfast table. When he came downstairs with his shirt on backward and his shoes missing, we still praised him. He had tried and was feeling good. Pointing out

WHENEVER POSSIBLE, DISH OUT PRAISE IN LARGE PORTIONS.

his shortcomings would have discouraged him. We encouraged his efforts instead.

Monitor your responses—positive and negative. Your positive responses are much more powerful than negative ones. Proverbs 16:24 reads, "Pleasant words are a honeycomb, sweet to the soul and healing to the bones." Whenever possible, dish out praise in large portions, especially when you see a positive action that results from previous discipline.

One mother wore a golf clicker on her arm for a day. Every time she made a negative comment, she clicked one side. She tracked her positive comments on the other. She was astonished to discover that her negative comments outnumbered her positive ones eight to one.

Principle 4: Think Long Term

I (Joanne) didn't just run to feel good every day. I ran because I wanted to be healthy. Regular exercise provides long-term benefits. Likewise, it's important for you to think long term as you discipline your children. You are building godly character that will provide the basis for their spiritual development. As you teach your children to submit, to show honor and respect, to be loving and kind, and so forth, you are laying the foundation for their long-term responsiveness to God.

"Train a child in the way he should go," we read in Proverbs 22:6, "and when he is old he will not turn from it." You are training your children for the future. You are not simply changing their behavior to make present circumstances easier. One reason children need to learn to obey their parents is so that they can obey God. Obedience is bigger than a parenting issue. It's a God issue. When your daughter's ball rolls into the street and she starts to run after it, you yell, "Stop!" You don't want her to evaluate your instruction. You want her to instinctively stop at the sound of your voice. This is the kind of obedience children need to develop so they will respond to God in the same way.

Parenthood is partnership with God. Our teaching of godly character provides the basis for spiritual development in our children. Key attitudes such as obedience, submission, and honor toward God are best learned as children and practiced throughout life.

Develop Your Own Flexible Philosophy of Discipline

When you're tired or you've solved too many problems already and you're faced with yet another challenge, having your own clear philosophy of discipline will motivate you to persevere and be consistent. Your calling as a parent will give you the ability to press on no matter what.

At various times in your children's growth, you will emphasize different things through your discipline. Some situations will work quite well. Others won't. Some types of discipline will work well with one child but not with another. There are no easy discipline "formulas" guaranteed to work in each child's life. So it's important to give yourself some grace, keep learning new things, and trust God to help you as you do the best you can.

Perhaps you feel like a failure because a child has developed rather difficult problems. If so, realize you are not alone! I (Scott) remember teaching my kids to work hard, earn money, and save. After a while, I began to see selfishness and materialism creep into their lives. At first, I thought, *Oh no, I've created little monsters.* Then, I realized I just needed to make a shift and emphasize a different quality—generosity.

By making this shift, I was able to give my children a more rounded approach to character development.

Perhaps your kids have developed some negative character traits along the way. If so, this is not a time for you to beat yourself up with guilt because of the way you've disciplined (or not disciplined). Make adjustments now, and begin to emphasize different things with your children. You'll see new changes that will help to round out their development.

Furthermore, you may discover that you're doing some great things that just aren't working. After all, parenting is a moving target. Just when you think things are rolling along with a child, he has a birthday, and a new set of problems arises. Strive to keep learning and stay on top of changes you need to make. Read new parenting books or reread old ones. Talk with other parents. Seek out a wise, godly counselor. You have many options!

Take Advantage of Parenting Differences

One challenge faced by families with more than one parent is the difference in parenting styles, particularly in discipline-related areas. The way parents discipline is based on their values and what they choose to emphasize at any given time.

One couple came in for counseling to address problems they saw in their six-year-old, Robert. As the dialogue continued, it became clear that some of the conflict existed because Mom and Dad disagreed about how to discipline. "At mealtime," one asked, "should we require him to sit straight and eat, or should we allow him to be silly with his brother?" The answer to that question has a lot to do with a philosophy of parenting. These parents encountered similar disagreements when addressing Robert's messy room, bad attitudes, and chores around the house.

Children can benefit from the convictions of both parents.

The discipline-related differences between Mom's way and Dad's way can help children develop a balanced perspective. Unfortunately, if parents don't acknowledge and accept each other's differences, they each will tend to overemphasize their own way in an attempt to "balance things out." In the end, they accentuate their differences, move further and further apart, end up feeling frustrated, and confuse their children.

We (Scott and Joanne) spent several weeks helping Robert's parents understand each other and learn to value each other's strengths. We found good points in both approaches to discipline and looked for ways to incorporate them into a philosophy of parenting. Both Mom and Dad agreed to tolerate a little silliness and de-emphasize manners for the sake of relationship and a positive mealtime. Dad felt uncomfortable at first but accepted the solution because he valued positive relationships with his children.

Sometimes parents can't come to an agreement, or one parent is unwilling to discuss value-related differences. This happens in traditional families but is most prevalent in single-parent or blended-family dynamics. If this is happening in your family, help the children deal with different philosophies of discipline. Explain your values and convictions. "I know that when you go to your dad's house," you might say, "he lets you eat junk food, watch violent movies, and doesn't make you clean up your room. I can't control what happens when you're over there, but I want you to understand why we have certain rules in this house."

Such an approach teaches children about your convictions and values—the foundation of your philosophy of discipline. Talking about values and convictions with kids helps them to understand differences and even gives them the foundation for making their own choices as they get older.

One twelve-year-old boy said, "My dad is pretty strict and sometimes I don't like that, but other times I think it's good. I've started going to bed at 9:30 at my mom's house on my own because I like being self-disciplined. My dad taught me that."

There are obviously many ways to discipline and raise children. Writing down your values and determining why you do what you do will help to guide you through day-to-day challenges. When you don't know what to do about a particular problem, ask yourself these important questions about the situation:

☐ What is it that I don't like about what happened here?
☐ What values drive me to that conclusion?
☐ What possible solutions might help, and which values lead me to those alternatives?

This work will help to clarify your philosophy of discipline. It will help you to understand more about what you want in your relationship with your kids. Also, an understanding of your philosophy of discipline will increase your sense of mission with your children and give you greater motivation to work with them.

It's Worth It!

Maintaining consistency in discipline is tough, but its payoffs are big! Although it requires a little forethought, the time and energy spent defining your philosophy of discipline will give you purpose, direction, and the motivation to hang in there. Here's a quick summary of the four principles that will help you stay on track even when you're feeling tired or overwhelmed.

1. Focus on the goals.
2. Endure the pain.
3. Look for ways to make it positive.
4. Think long term.

Chapter 7

Teaching Kids to Learn from Life

Marlene sat at the dining-room table, her eyes growing larger as she listened to her sister's stories. Linda had recently returned from a short-term mission trip to Kenya and was describing the time her team went to a tribal village to help build a church. Marlene enjoyed hearing about the way God worked there.

Jennifer came into the room. "Mom, I'm hungry."

Marlene sighed. "Jennifer, I'll get you something in a few minutes." She looked at Linda. "I guess I better get up and make a snack."

Danny burst through the front door. "Mom, I can't find my baseball glove!"

"I just saw it somewhere. Let me look." Marlene jumped up and headed down the hall. *I wish I could just sit and listen to Linda, but these kids always need something.*

After a few minutes, Danny ran back outside. Jennifer finished her snack and wandered back to her room. Marlene brought a bowl of carrot sticks to the table.

"Having children looks demanding." Linda smiled.

"It sure is." Marlene took a deep breath. "These two always want something from me."

"They do bring a lot of their problems to you. Do *you* always have to solve them?"

"What do you mean?"

"It just seems to me that they rely pretty heavily on you. When I was in Kenya, I was impressed by the amount of work and responsibility the children have there."

"Well, this isn't Kenya, and I'm their mother. It's my job to help them."

"I suppose, but don't you think they might learn more from solving their own problems?"

"They're only eight and four. They need me."

"Sure, but do they need you *that* much?" Linda continued, a touch of teasing in her voice. "I bet Jennifer could have gotten a snack without your help."

"Maybe."

"And Danny's baseball glove was right on his bed. He just hadn't looked carefully."

"I know, but he was frustrated, and I was trying to help him."

"Yes, but maybe you rescued him too soon. A little gentle encouragement might have been all he needed." Concerned that she had overstepped her bounds, Linda continued carefully. "Hey, I'm not a parent, but I care about my baby sister, and she's looking pretty exhausted right now. Just think about what I said, okay?"

I like to solve the kids' problems, but it does get tiring after a while. "I appreciate your looking out for me. Thanks, Sis."

After Linda left, Marlene thought about her interactions with the kids. Her sister was right. Jennifer and Danny often expected her to do things they could do for themselves.

"Mom, I can't find my barrette."

"Mom, my shoelace has a knot."

"Mom, the toilet paper's gone."

"Mom, Jennifer is playing with my puzzle."

Marlene began to see that the children continually looked to her to solve simple problems. Jennifer and Danny could do much more for themselves if she would step aside more often and allow them to struggle a little.

That evening Craig leaned against the kitchen counter, listening to his wife. "So you're saying that the kids don't know how to solve their own problems?"

Marlene nodded. "Either that, or they don't want to. I didn't really notice until Linda said something. The more I think about it, the more I think she's right."

"What are you going to do about it?"

"Well, I'm not sure. First, I want to know what you think."

"What you're saying makes sense. If we could get them to solve some of their problems, it would help us, and it might help them grow up a little. Maybe they've learned that all they have to do is tell us their problems, and we'll solve them. If they complain about something, we usually try to make it better."

"Wow. I don't like the way that sounds, but maybe it's true. It's as if we've taught them to complain about things they don't like. We definitely have to change *that*."

"At least when they bring a problem to us," said Craig, "they could ask for help instead of just complaining. Instead of saying, 'I'm hungry,' with that whiny voice, Jennifer could say, 'Mom, could I please have a snack?'; or Danny could ask for help instead of just complaining about not being able to find something. Then they'd both be taking a little responsibility for the solutions."

"I like that," Marlene agreed. "We can tell them that if they're just expressing a problem, they're complaining. They need to try to offer solutions."

She thought for a moment. "But won't they feel as if I don't care about them if I tell them I'm not going to solve all their problems? After all, I am their mom. It seems so cold to just tell them to go and solve problems themselves."

"Maybe, but I think teaching them to solve more of their problems is a loving thing to do."

"I guess you're right. Let's give it a try."

The next day, Marlene looked for opportunities to help the kids solve their problems on their own. At one point, Jennifer came into the kitchen and complained that she was hungry.

"Jennifer, it sounds as if you're complaining. 'Hungry' is the problem. What's the solution?"

Jennifer paused. "What? I'm hungry."

"I'm trying to teach you how to solve problems and not just complain about them. Think of what you want, and, if you need help, ask me instead of just telling me what's wrong."

"Uh ... I want a snack."

"Okay. So why don't you go back into the hallway and come into the kitchen again. Then you can ask me nicely without complaining."

Jennifer stepped outside the kitchen, turned around, and came back in. "Mom, could I please have a snack?"

"That was great. You got rid of the complaining and focused on the solution instead. Thank you. What would you like?"

"I don't know."

"Why don't you come up with an idea and try again? You can be the problem solver."

Jennifer thought a minute, then asked, "Could I have an apple?"

"Okay, I think that's a good idea. Go get an apple."

Later Danny couldn't find his red rubber ball. Marlene said, "I know how it feels when you lose something that's important to you. It sure is frustrating, isn't it?"

"Could you find it, Mom?"

"I'm sorry, but I can't do that right now. I'm cooking dinner. I can help you in about fifteen minutes, or maybe this is a problem you can solve yourself. Would you like an idea?"

"But I already looked."

"Well, sometimes if you just sit and think about where you had it last, you may remember, or you may want to go back to the places you normally play with it."

"I know!" Danny replied. "I'll go look in the backyard. It might be there."

A minute later, he found the ball by the back door and marched triumphantly into the kitchen to show his mom.

Marlene smiled. *I like this. It's fun to watch Danny succeed. He looks so proud of himself.*

That evening when Craig got home from work, he asked Marlene how her day had been.

"Well, I had a few chances to help Jennifer and Danny solve their problems on their own."

"Really? Did it work?"

"Sometimes, and that was great. But some problems aren't as easy to fix as others. Jennifer's friend Karissa was being mean, and Jennifer didn't handle it well. I need to think about more ways to help her deal with that kind of problem by herself."

"That makes sense."

"What I like about this new approach, though, is that it helps them develop a sense of responsibility for their problems—and it teaches them to think creatively instead of just giving up."

"I think we've discovered another tool," Craig said with a smile.

Using Tool 7: A Parent Who Is a Counselor or Coach Enables Children to Learn from Life

Kids like to bring their problems to Mom and Dad for solutions. Sometimes this is appropriate. A young child who wants to cut up an apple or a teenager who needs a ride home from an activity should receive help from a parent. When children are young, they need to bring important problems to their parents because they're not yet mature enough to solve them. But as kids grow older, many problems they bring to their parents represent opportunities to seek solutions by themselves.

Experience is a valuable teacher. It teaches skills such as how to ride a bike, how to find lost shoes, and how to pay for something at the store. Experience teaches children what it feels like to be left out, to win or lose, or to be put on the spot. Experience can teach character qualities such as courage to try new foods, patience with a younger sibling, or perseverance to complete a project. But it's seldom easy to learn from experiences—particularly, challenging or painful ones.

Unfortunately, though, if parents aren't careful, they can rob their children of lessons that could be learned from experience because they believe that loving their kids means keeping them from struggles. Parents who continually rescue their children often short-circuit the learning process by intervening too soon.

Sometimes parents can accomplish more by doing less. When kids have to work through their problems on their own, experience becomes the teacher and parents function as the counselors or coaches. Many parents don't realize the benefit of allowing children to experience the consequences of their actions. Wanting to spare their kids from struggles, these parents step in unnecessarily and rob their children of excellent ways to learn key values, principles, and habits.

One dad bought a new package of batteries for his twelve-year-old daughter, Meg. She began to rip at the package, but the combination of cardboard and plastic seemed impregnable. "How are you supposed to get these batteries out of here?" she asked.

Dad could feel his daughter's frustration but didn't want to solve the problem for her. Rather than give her the answer, he affirmed her by saying, "I think you have to be a detective to get into these new kinds of packages."

That was all Meg needed. She stopped tugging and looked at the package more carefully. After finding the tab that said "pull here," she successfully opened the package. Sacrificing the benefit he would have felt from rescuing his daughter, Dad felt the internal satisfaction of encouraging her to solve the problem herself.

WHEN ALLOWING CHILDREN TO SOLVE THEIR OWN PROBLEMS, IT'S IMPORTANT TO MONITOR THEIR FRUSTRATION LEVEL.

When allowing children to solve their own problems, it's important to monitor the frustration level. A little frustration, overcome by persistence, builds determination. Too much frustration causes discouragement. Coaching children through the problem-solving process requires patience and sensitivity.

The challenge of helping children to solve problems by themselves is complicated by the fact that we as parents don't want to appear uncaring in our approach. Just telling kids to solve their own problems can seem insensitive. So let's explore ways in which we can equip our children to solve problems—and express our love at the same time. Our children will gain greater confidence as they solve problems and come to view us as counselors and coaches.

Ask Open-ended Questions

A primary tool for helping children to solve problems for themselves is asking open-ended questions, such as "What's the matter?"; "What's it supposed to look like?"; "What are you going to do about it?" Open-ended questions help children learn a process for solving problems, give the responsibility for problems back to the children, and help them grow and mature.

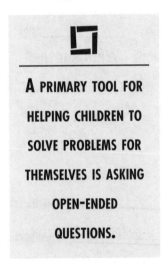

A PRIMARY TOOL FOR HELPING CHILDREN TO SOLVE PROBLEMS FOR THEMSELVES IS ASKING OPEN-ENDED QUESTIONS.

Jesus was a master at guiding people in this way. "What do you want me to do for you?" he asked the two blind men who were sitting by the roadside (Matt. 20:32). "Who do people say the Son of Man is?" and "Who do you say I am?" he asked the disciples (Matt. 16:13, 15). By asking open-ended questions, Jesus often moved to a deeper level with people, helping them to think for themselves.

If six-year-old Paul announces at dinner, "I don't have a fork," Mom may be tempted to get up and get one for him. But instead of solving this problem for him, she may wisely respond by saying, "I see you have a problem, Paul. What do you think you ought to do about it?"

Some parents feel that just reflecting the problem back to their children isn't loving. They think, *I just couldn't do that. It doesn't seem right.* Sometimes, though, the loving response is to demonstrate confidence in your children's ability to solve their problems. Rather than turning their backs and walking away, thoughtful parents can help children evaluate choices, offer suggestions, and give praise for accomplishments. Children grow in confidence as they learn to overcome challenges for themselves.

Paul may decide that a fork isn't necessary and be content to use a spoon. Then, his mom or dad could praise him for his flexibility. He may get up to get one out of the drawer only to discover that all the forks are gone. After all, solving problems isn't always easy. He may find a clean one not yet put away or choose to wash a fork that's dirty. A key is to offer just enough guidance to allow the child to feel the accomplishment of problem solving.

Steps for Using Open-ended Questions

Here are six steps for using open-ended questions to help children solve problems for themselves.

Step 1: Encourage Discussion

When children respond to open-ended questions by saying, "I don't know," be careful about launching into a lecture. Lectures can hinder the process of discovery, yet it's amazing how some children bait their parents into lectures. These children know just what to say to provoke their parents into making eloquent speeches, then resist or even complain. (It's always easier to complain about someone else's ideas than to develop your own.)

If this occurs in your family, be careful that you don't get sucked in. Lectures are helpful if children want to learn. If they don't, lectures have little value, and personal experience may be a better teacher.

Frustration can be a sign that tells you a good opportunity for learning is coming. Each child handles frustration differently. One frustrated child will come to a parent about an issue. Another will just live with the frustration of an unsolved problem. Yet another will try to solve the

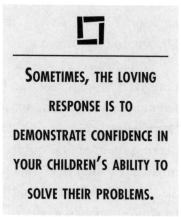

SOMETIMES, THE LOVING RESPONSE IS TO DEMONSTRATE CONFIDENCE IN YOUR CHILDREN'S ABILITY TO SOLVE THEIR PROBLEMS.

problem but may not have the wisdom to do it properly. When frustration surfaces, be careful not to lecture. You might miss a great teaching opportunity. A guided discussion is often more productive.

Sometimes caring involves seeing a child's frustration and taking initiative. Dad may see Alex withdraw from other children and say, "Alex, it looks like you're having a problem. Come tell me about it." As Alex shares his struggle, Dad can then use more questions to explore the problem and gently help his son find possible solutions.

Step 2: Express Sincere Empathy

If you leave out this step, children may react poorly to your open-ended questions. They may view your approach as condescending or cold and respond with anger or hostility. Empathy communicates love while allowing children to take responsibility for problem solving.

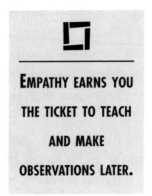

EMPATHY EARNS YOU THE TICKET TO TEACH AND MAKE OBSERVATIONS LATER.

Instead of asking rhetorical questions that just make a point such as "Kyle, you missed the bus; what are you going to do tomorrow?" take a moment to connect on an emotional level. "Kyle, I know how you don't like to be late. Missing the bus was a tough way to start the day."

Empathy earns you the ticket to teach and make observations later. If your children feel understood, they will be more willing to discuss solutions and listen to what you have to say. Connecting with your children's emotions is often the key to making open-ended questions work as a teaching tool. You might say, "I bet that feels terrible," "I understand why you're discouraged," "I'd feel bad if that happened to me," or "Your frustration makes sense."

Empathy may be hard if the emotion your child is experiencing is anger and you're angry, too. One mom said, "I realized that my goal in the conversation was to resolve my own anger, so I said things that weren't all that helpful. Now I try to imagine how my daughter's feeling and look for ways to connect with her on that level."

Step 3: Get Permission to Share Alternatives

If your child has no idea how to solve a particular problem, you may want to offer suggestions. Sometimes though, children (and adults) share their problems because they want sympathy, not solutions. If you sense that's the case, move back to step 2 and express empathy. In fact, your role in this particular situation may simply be to come alongside and care.

Try to discern whether your child is ready to hear possible solutions. Asking permission is an excellent way to do this. You might say, "Would you like an idea?" or "Would you like to hear how other people might solve this problem?" Timing is very important. Children who are ready to discuss solutions will often provide the direction you need to know how you should proceed next in the dialogue.

One mom said, "When I ask my kids if they want some ideas, it sets the stage for us to brainstorm together. If I just start giving ideas, it seems that I'm intruding or talking down to them. When I ask permission, then they're much more open with me."

Step 4: List Several Alternatives

Depending on your child's responsiveness, you may want to share the worst alternative first. After all, unhappy kids often look at the negative side of solutions. There's no point wasting your good ideas when bad attitudes rule. You might say to ten-year-old Katie, "Let's see, you're angry with Tara, so you could cancel the sleepover this weekend."

"No, I don't want to do that," she might reply.

"Okay," you might answer. "Maybe we could work this out a different way. What do you think about telling her that you don't like what she did?"

As you discuss each alternative together, help your child anticipate the consequences of each. After sharing a possible solution, you may ask, "What might happen if you do that?" Anticipating consequences helps your child learn to think through each alternative carefully.

A good problem-solving process helps participants recognize where possible solutions may lead. In fact, the whole point of allowing children to learn from experience is to teach them about life. Evaluating consequences helps your children grow in wisdom.

Fourteen-year-old Bobby wanted to buy a remote-control car from his friend for a hundred dollars. Although a new remote-control car cost twice that much, this one wasn't working properly. Bobby had ideas of how to fix it, but Mom had doubts. Wanting to let Bobby make the decision, she used open-ended questions to help them discuss key issues.

Step 5: Allow the Child to Choose a Solution

After you've given your counsel, let your child make a choice. As much as possible, avoid solving problems for children that they can solve themselves. After you've brainstormed possible alternatives, you may ask, "What are you going to do now?" or "Which one of these choices seems like the best one for you?" Then allow the child to think about the situation. Many children need prompting to make a decision. It's this step that keeps them moving in the right direction.

As Bobby and his mother explored alternatives, he decided to ask his friend to fix the car before he bought it. Mom was willing to allow Bobby to purchase the unrepaired car, but she was relieved when he decided to wait.

One day my (Scott) daughter Melissa, age nine, came to me

with a problem, saying, "My friend wants to play with me but wants to exclude another girl I also want to play with."

"Oh, that's sad," I said. "What are you going to do?"

After thinking for a minute, she replied, "I'm just going to tell her if she wants to play with me, then she'll have to accept the other girl too."

"That sounds like it might work. Why don't you try it and let me know how it goes."

My initial thought was to tell Melissa how to solve her problem, but my use of questions enabled her to come to a solution herself. I became the counselor.

Step 6: Recognize That Sometimes Good Solutions Are Elusive

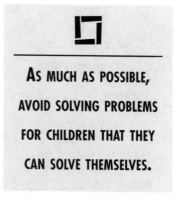

AS MUCH AS POSSIBLE, AVOID SOLVING PROBLEMS FOR CHILDREN THAT THEY CAN SOLVE THEMSELVES.

Life is hard. Sometimes all possible solutions seem bleak, and children may not like any of the solutions. For example, let's say you have a son named Jacob. It's raining, and Jacob's soccer game is canceled. He's disappointed. You've expressed empathy and discussed alternative activities, but Jacob seems more interested in complaining and having a bad attitude than in finding a solution.

At this point, you have another teaching opportunity. You might say, "I've tried to help you with this problem. I understand that you're upset. I'm not sure what else to do. I know that sometimes kids like to be sad, and other times they like to be happy. That's a choice you need to make, but I don't want you to mistreat me in the process with your bad attitude. I think it would be good for you to play by yourself for a while, think about whether you want to be happy or sad, and figure out what else you'd like to do."

Complaining, which continues to focus on a problem without acknowledging or taking responsibility for the solution, is unacceptable. Don't take responsibility for a child's problem when he or she just wants to focus on the negative.

Sometimes in this situation, parents try to relieve the pain of disappointment by providing other forms of entertainment. Although this isn't necessarily wrong, parents should not feel responsible for making kids happy after life has dealt them some disappointment. They need to learn contentment and flexibility in life. Disappointment is inevitable, and we all need to learn how to deal with it.

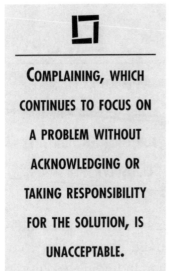

COMPLAINING, WHICH CONTINUES TO FOCUS ON A PROBLEM WITHOUT ACKNOWLEDGING OR TAKING RESPONSIBILITY FOR THE SOLUTION, IS UNACCEPTABLE.

That said, allow me (Scott) to tell a story about when my children were disappointed and how I responded.

One afternoon Josh and Melissa came into my office, plopped down, and announced, "We're bored, and it's your fault."

I was busy, but their words sparked my interest. I turned around and said, "Tell me about it."

"Well, all the other kids in the neighborhood are in school. We're finished with our work. You chose to homeschool us. So we're bored, and it's your fault."

I felt like saying, "Wait just a moment," then running upstairs to get more schoolwork. Instead, I said empathetically, "So you're bored. You wish you had something fun to do, right?"

"Yes," they agreed.

"Would you like to know how other people might solve this problem?" I asked.

"All right."

"Okay. Let me think of some categories of things that you might do—besides being entertained or getting into mischief."

The list we came up with that day is what our family uses to this day to combat boredom. After listing the possibilities, I said, "Why don't you two talk about it and let me know what you're going to do." After a brief discussion, they decided to build a fort in the backyard, and it kept them occupied most of the afternoon.

How to Use Natural Consequences Effectively

One of the goals we parents have for our children is to help them become independent, responsible adults. As we've already seen, the way parents discipline can prepare children for life. Sometimes, though, the best way to help our children is to do nothing and stay out of the way, allowing natural consequences to provide the teaching.

We sometimes become uneasy with our children's frustration in a given situation and step in too early, short-circuiting the learning process.

SIX THINGS TO DO WHEN YOU'RE BORED

1. Be Creative—Use art, music, or drama. Make a project, or just think of new ways to solve a problem. Creativity can be fun, fulfilling, and restful.

2. Build Relationships—Write a letter, talk to people, call someone on the phone, ask questions, or meet someone new.

3. Serve Others—At first, children may think this is just more work. But if they can catch a vision for pleasing others or ministering to them, then this can be a great activity. Ideas include baking cookies for the family, babysitting for some neighborhood children, or raking leaves off the neighbor's lawn.

4. Self-improvement—Practice a skill, read a book, learn something, memorize a Bible verse, or organize your desk.

5. Rest—This is not usually high on the list, but it's sometimes helpful. Boredom is often the result of being too tired to do anything else.

6. The Imagination Factor—God has given you a brain that has no limit to the ideas you can come up with to solve the boredom problem.

Instead, there are times when we should change roles. We can view ourselves as counselors or coaches and let life teach our children valuable lessons. When we intentionally stay out of problems and make little or no comment, our children have opportunities to learn from life.

The apostle Peter experienced the natural consequence of lack of faith when he stepped out of the boat and began to sink. (See Matt. 14.) Jesus, the Counselor, then helped him. Jesus also allowed Peter to make the mistake of denying him three times. No lectures or rebukes were needed—just a look from the Master's eyes and Peter was overcome with remorse. (See Luke 22.) Many times, Jesus allowed life to be the teacher and took on a supportive role.

Children who can't take responsibility for their mistakes especially need to learn about natural consequences. These children, who tend to blame other people who try to help them, need more reality checks. These reality checks often come when the children experience the consequences of their mistakes. When life is allowed to be the teacher, children often learn that their actions produce consequences.

When natural consequences occur, our response can affect how much our children actually learn from a given situation. Following are four steps that will help you use natural consequences more effectively.

Step 1: Offer Fewer Instructions and Warnings

Natural consequences work best when parents can keep quiet and not intervene, allowing life to be the teacher. So parents must learn to discern how much to encourage or teach in any given situation. Too many times, parents believe it's their obligation to step in and prevent or point out errors. Using natural consequences, parents realize that they don't have to speak in order for their children to learn.

The five-year-old who goes out to play on a hot day wearing

a turtleneck learns a lesson. The ten-year-old who spends all his money on one thing may wish he had not done so. The sixteen-year-old who puts off doing her laundry may be disappointed in a few days when she has no clean jeans. Each of these experiences can become a learning opportunity if parents respond wisely.

It's helpful, though, to model wise behavior. You may say to an eight-year-old, "It's going to be cool later. I'm going to take a sweater." Or say to a five-year-old, "I'm going to eat a snack now, since dinner won't be for a couple of hours."

Sometimes, of course, it's helpful to mention possible consequences, but allow the child to choose. "If you spend your last ten dollars, you won't have any money when another opportunity comes around." A gentle warning that appreciates the child's abilities can go a long way. But too much talking removes opportunities for children to learn from their experiences.

Step 2: Communicate Genuine Empathy When Natural Consequences Occur

When your child begins to experience natural consequences, be empathetic. You may say, "Yes, it's sad that your markers got all dried out. I guess those caps are important." Or, "Ouch! I'm sorry you stubbed your toe. I bet that hurts."

Empathy contributes to positive relationships. You don't want your children to feel guilty when they make less-than-perfect decisions on their own. On the contrary, you want them to learn from their mistakes and go on in life. Your response can either foster their confidence or damage it.

One man in his early twenties said, "I see that there are two kinds of people in life: those who take risks and those who don't. Some people have to know everything before they make a decision. I have the courage to step out when others are hesitant. I thank my mom for her encouragement as I was growing up. She had faith in me." That's the kind of confidence you build into your children when you allow them to learn from life. But don't just encourage their positive decisions. You must also empathize with their poor decisions as you try to motivate them toward maturity.

Step 3: Avoid Rescuing or Condemning

Avoid saying, "I told you so," when a negative consequence occurs. Such a statement only serves to emphasize guilt or condemnation. The temptation is huge, though, so be careful that you don't build yourself up at your child's expense. Work with the child to explore the results of a situation and what might have been done differently.

AVOID SAYING, "I TOLD YOU SO," WHEN A NEGATIVE CONSEQUENCE OCCURS.

Also, as we've already touched on, don't step in too quickly to relieve consequences and thereby short-circuit the learning process. Rescuing teaches valuable lessons about parental love and faithfulness, but that's not the only choice.

Let's say that your child leaves something important at home and heads off for school. Do you take that paper, lunch, or book to school—or allow the child to experience the negative consequences? Yes, we all forget things at times, and part of being in a family means that we look out for each other. But if your child continually forgets things, natural consequences may help to develop maturity.

Our children need the freedom to make mistakes. When we allow them to experience negative consequences, we may be giving them gifts. In essence, we're saying to our children that we believe in them, that we know they can and will make adjustments and learn from life's experiences.

Step 4: Discuss Resulting Consequences During Teachable Moments

After the consequence of your child's action is recognized, determine whether you have a teachable moment with him or her. Sometimes a brief discussion is helpful, but you don't have to lecture. You may simply make an observation, not expecting a response. You may say, "It looks like your silliness went a little too far," or "Next time you might want to move your puzzle, so someone doesn't accidentally bump it." Don't wait around for an answer or response. Your observation is the statement of reality that helps your child interpret the life lesson.

Avoid engaging in an argument. If you can leave the conversation with an observation for your child to consider, you'll get further than encouraging an intense word exchange. Remember, you don't have to provide a lesson or prove a point. With a natural consequence, life is the teacher.

When Not to Use Natural Consequences

As useful and effective as natural consequences can be, they are not always appropriate and may even be dangerous. Natural consequences should be discontinued when property is in danger, when the child may get hurt or hurt others, or when undue frustration may result in discouragement. Furthermore, if the child is not learning from the natural consequence, use another approach.

A parent may hope that fourteen-year-old George will grow tired of his messy room and develop a desire to keep it clean. However, the natural consequence may not motivate him to be neat. The parent then may choose a different approach.

A parent may become frustrated with a child and say, "Fine. I'm just going to let him learn for himself." This attempt to use natural consequences is okay if it has the potential to promote growth in the child's life. But sometimes doing this will only lead to more failure.

For example, a child who is doing poorly at school and neglecting to turn in homework assignments is unlikely to respond to natural consequences. Instead, he or she is grateful that the parent isn't requiring action steps, and the child will most likely continue to fail.

On the other hand, a high achiever at school may accept a social activity on the night before a big test. You may choose to allow the poor choice, recognizing the bind the child is creating. The hope is that the natural consequence of feeling the pressure of schoolwork will teach him or her to limit other good things in order to be responsible. This may be an effective use of a natural consequence.

The use of natural consequences assumes that a certain level of motivation exists for the children to pursue a solution. The children have to want to succeed.

Children who are not motivated to succeed or are stuck in a cycle of failure don't need natural consequences. They need a boot-camp experience in order to develop such character qualities as perseverance, thoroughness, and responsibility.

The use of natural consequences takes advantage of an important principle about wisdom. Wisdom foresees the consequences of actions. All people—parents and children—need to grow in wisdom in life, but children often don't see consequences early enough in the process. As a parent, you know that teasing can get out of hand and someone will get hurt. You see that flying the kite too close to the trees risks losing the kite. Children often can't see those things in advance. Wisdom comes from experience. Used properly, natural consequences help children to grow in maturity.

Logical Consequences

In contrast to natural consequences, logical consequences permit children to learn about the real world through simulated consequences. Use them in place of natural consequences to prevent people or property from damage and/or to speed up the learning process.

The natural consequence of leaving a bike out in the rain is a rusted bike that eventually will become inoperable. Because rusting would take years, you can use a logical consequence to speed up the process. The outcome of a rusted bike is that the child wouldn't be able to ride it, so you may say, "Amy, if you leave your bike out, you won't be allowed to ride it tomorrow." This is a logical consequence that speeds up the natural consequence in order to teach Amy that, when she doesn't take care of her bike, she'll eventually lose the privilege of riding it.

Whereas natural consequences simply require that the parent "get out of the way," logical consequences often require thoughtfulness and preplanning. When choosing a logical consequence, first ask yourself, *What might eventually happen if this behavior were allowed to continue?*

It's no secret that guiding children during the process of maturity requires great perseverance on your part. Hang in there. Continue to discipline consistently. Look for ways to use natural and logical consequences that will have great impact. And pray hard. As parents, we are only one of the influences in our children's lives, albeit a significant one. God loves them, too, and he has many more resources to help them. Just as he allowed natural consequences to teach the Israelites during their forty years in the wilderness, God can teach your children. Pray that he will do the deeper work necessary to build lasting character in them.

God wants to bless your children. Your training can go a long way to prepare your son or daughter for God's continued work. There are few things more rewarding than watching children grow up to be adults of character and godliness.

It's Worth It!

By using open-ended questions, natural consequences, and logical consequences, parents provide children with opportunities to learn from life. These discipline approaches sometimes take more patience or planning, but they are well worth the extra effort.

Here's a quick summary of how to use open-ended questions and natural and logical consequences effectively.

To use open-ended questions effectively,

- encourage discussion,
- express sincere empathy,
- get permission to share alternatives,
- list several alternatives,
- allow the child to choose a solution, and
- recognize that sometimes good solutions are elusive.

To use natural consequences effectively,

- offer fewer instructions and warnings,
- communicate genuine empathy when natural consequences occur,
- avoid rescuing or condemning, and
- discuss resulting consequences during teachable moments.

Use logical consequences in place of natural consequences to prevent people or property from damage and/or to speed up the learning process.

Chapter 8

Approaching Deep-rooted Problems

Craig opened the Saturday paper and settled back on the living-room couch. Danny and Jennifer played in the other room, seemingly content to put together the train set and a community of toy people. Having just finished a wild twenty minutes of bear-hunt and wrestling time, Craig hoped to catch up on the latest news before getting ready for dinner guests.

Marlene walked into the living room and picked up a large picture book lying on the floor. "I wish we could do something about the mess these kids make," she said. "They leave things all over the house. It seems as if they never put anything away. I find toys scattered everywhere, and most puzzles and games have pieces missing. They leave coats and shoes wherever they take them off. I have to follow them around and pick up after them, or you wouldn't even be able to walk—"

"Okay, I get the picture." Craig interrupted with a smile. "What time are the Wongs coming?"

"About six thirty." Marlene sighed, looking at the messy living room.

"All right. Give me five more minutes, and then I'll help pick up while you finish dinner."

"Thanks. Could you start with the bathroom?" Marlene placed the book on the shelf and walked to the kitchen.

Craig scanned the front page and the sports section, then

folded the paper and headed for the bathroom. After cleaning there, he quickly straightened up in the living room and entryway. With a satisfied glance over his shoulder, he entered the kitchen. "Want me to set the table?"

"Sure, that would be great."

Craig took six plates from the cabinet. "I'm looking forward to seeing the Wongs tonight."

"Me, too. It'll be nice to spend time with a couple who've been married as long as they have." Marlene opened the oven to check the casserole.

"Yeah, they did a great job with their kids, too. Both their boys are committed to the Lord and raising families of their own. I'm sure we could learn a lot from them."

"Well, maybe they'll share some of their secrets," Marlene added.

Soon, Bill and Esther arrived. Craig and Marlene greeted them warmly and invited them in. After everybody sat down at the table, Craig thanked God for the food, and they all began eating.

Bill engaged Danny and Jennifer in the conversation by asking them several questions. The children answered politely and seemed to be on their best behavior, much to their parents' relief.

Esther smiled across the table at Craig and Marlene. "You know, it's been a long time since our children were this age. Our boys were full of energy and excitement just like Jennifer and Danny. Sometimes our house seems pretty quiet now that it's just the two of us."

"I imagine it does," Marlene said. "You're in a completely different stage of life than we are. Most of our family life revolves around the kids."

Esther nodded. "These formative years are very important. I know you want to make the most of them."

Esther's comment hit home with Craig. *I often get so caught up in the day-to-day rush of life that I don't even consider how quickly the kids are growing up.*

After dinner, Craig put the kids to bed while the others cleared the table. When he returned, he sighed and sat down on the couch next to Marlene. "Things sure do quiet down once the kids are in bed," he stated.

"Yes, parenting is hard work," Bill replied. "But I'm sure you realize that if you work at it now, your efforts will pay off."

"We've definitely been working hard at it lately," Marlene said, pouring tea. "Craig and I have learned several important things about parenting these past few months."

Esther took a cup from the tray. "Is that right? What have you been learning?"

As Craig and Marlene talked about their new discipline strategies, Bill and Esther listened intently. Craig shared about how a tight Action Point was helping the children learn that they needed to obey quickly. He also talked about the Positive Conclusion and how they were using rules to teach values.

"You're learning a number of things that many parents never understand," Bill said. "I like your emphasis on values and help-ing children to address heart issues."

Marlene sighed. "We've learned a lot about parenting, but sometimes I just don't see the changes I'd like to see in our chil-dren. It seems as if we're not getting through."

"Behavior is often a symptom of what's in the heart," Bill continued. "As parents, we want to help our children to develop godly character that in turn will lead to godly actions. Sometimes our discipline needs to focus on problems that are more deeply rooted in the heart."

"Yes," Craig said, "I know that building character is good, but it's hard to measure. We tend to focus on behavior because it's something we can see. If we try to develop character, how do we know if we're making progress?"

"That's a good question," Esther replied. "Here's an example. The phrase 'don't lie' focuses on behavior, while 'honesty' is a character quality that comes from the heart. As parents, we want to foster changes and help our children develop positive attitudes on this deeper level. We can then measure growth in character by observing behavior. The behavior we see is a reflection of what's going on in children's hearts. With our family, we found it helpful to focus on specific character qualities as our boys were growing up."

"I don't think Jennifer and Danny are old enough for that," Craig said. "I think they'd have a hard time understanding what many of the character qualities are, let alone knowing how to develop them."

Bill nodded. "It's helpful to define character qualities in practical ways that even young children can understand. Parents we've worked with have come up with some pretty good character-quality definitions through the years. Do you remember any of them, Esther?"

Esther thought for a moment. "One mom, concerned that her daughter wasn't looking at her when she was talking, defined *attentiveness* as 'showing people you love them by looking at them when they talk.' Another child was struggling with frustration when asked to wait, so her mom defined *patience* as 'waiting with a happy heart.' *Promptness* is 'showing someone you love them by valuing their time.'"

Bill continued. "It gets to be fun after a while. These working definitions give children specific things to do to develop each character quality. When our son Joseph was learning to play the piano, we defined *perseverance* as 'continuing to work hard even after you feel like quitting.' You see, perseverance doesn't begin until after you feel like quitting."

"I like that," said Craig. "It reminds me of our definition of obedience. We say *obedience* is 'doing what someone says, right away, without being reminded.'"

"Yes, that's the right idea," said Esther. "It's helpful to express the solution in a positive way, using a character quality and a definition that's easy to understand."

"I wonder if this could apply to cleaning up the house," Marlene said jokingly.

"What do you mean?" Esther asked.

"We were talking earlier this afternoon about how the children often leave things around the house and don't clean up after themselves."

"I can sure understand that." Esther smiled. "Children can be pretty selfish. That's exactly the kind of issue I think character addresses. Long-term or deep-rooted problems need to be addressed by a character-development plan. I'm sure there's a character quality that could help with messiness."

Marlene thought for a moment. "It seems like it's just being responsible to put away the things you got out … or maybe it's being loving to clean up the mess in the bathroom."

"Maybe we should call it thoughtfulness," Craig said.

"Usually more than one character quality addresses a particular problem," Bill added, "but it's helpful to pick one to emphasize."

"I like the idea of thoughtfulness for the bathroom problem," Marlene agreed. "How could we define it in a way that our children will understand?"

After a few moments, Esther suggested, "Maybe you could say that thoughtfulness is thinking about other people."

"Or thoughtfulness is making the bathroom ready for the next person," added Bill.

"I like that idea," affirmed Marlene. "I'm not sure how Jennifer and Danny will respond to it, though."

Esther took another sip of tea. "Character isn't developed overnight. I'm sure you'll find other ways to teach thoughtfulness, too. The important thing is for children to recognize the problem, understand that positive change is needed, and learn how to work on it. God continues the deeper work in their hearts."

After they said good-bye to the Wongs, Craig and Marlene continued to think about ideas for teaching thoughtfulness to their kids.

The next morning, Craig put a little sign in the bathroom that read, "Did you check to see if the bathroom is ready for the next person?" Then he called the whole family in to see the sign. "This is a reminder for all of us to be thoughtful to others," he said. "What kinds of things do you think we should check?"

"To see if the toilet's flushed," suggested Danny.

"Hang up the towel when we're done, and turn off the light," added Jennifer.

"Those are good suggestions. We could also add making sure the counter is wiped off and that things aren't on the floor. Let's see how we do with these ideas."

Later that day, Danny said, "Dad, I cleaned up the bathroom."

Craig's eyebrows went up. "You did? Show me."

Danny eagerly led his father into the bathroom.

"Wow! This does look clean."

"I straightened the rug and wiped out the sink."

"That's great, Danny. Thank you. I like the way you're being thoughtful in the bathroom. Let's go tell Mom."

Craig smiled. *Danny is getting the idea. It seems like all he needs is a little guidance in the right direction, and then he's ready to grow.*

Using Tool 8: Building a God-centered Character-development Plan

This tool is nicknamed the "Secret Weapon." Although you can use it anytime, you can implement this plan when all else seems to have failed.

The preceding chapters have established a framework for dealing with many discipline-related problems and preventing others that might otherwise occur. But no matter how hard we work at facing and resolving problems with our children, from time to time, deep-rooted patterns of behavior still need to be addressed. Normal day-to-day plans aren't enough to handle these big issues. We need to exert some concentrated effort in order to influence and, hopefully, change deeper issues of the heart.

In Matthew 23, Jesus criticized the Pharisees for cleaning the outside of the cup and dish (their outward behavior) but leaving the inside of the cup (their hearts) full of greed and self-indulgence. Jesus told them to first clean the inside of the cup so that the outside would also become clean. We need to work toward allowing God to change our children's hearts, not just focus on changing their behavior. Since this challenge

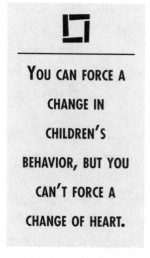

YOU CAN FORCE A CHANGE IN CHILDREN'S BEHAVIOR, BUT YOU CAN'T FORCE A CHANGE OF HEART.

can seem overwhelming, it's helpful to formulate a specific plan that uses a multifaceted approach—beginning with prayer.

Pray for your kids regularly. Although you can force a change in children's behavior, you can't force a change of heart. God is the one who changes hearts. David prayed, "Create in me a pure heart, O God" (Ps. 51:10) and acknowledged that God "knows the secrets of the heart" (Ps. 44:21).

As you pray for your children, several things happen. First, God works directly in your children's hearts as a result of your prayers. Also, your prayers raise your awareness level of God's work in your children's hearts. You see, some of the work God wants to do in them, he will do through you. If you are praying regularly for them, you will become more sensitive to issues and opportunities you face during the day that can make a big difference in your children's lives.

For example, we parents often react angrily to our children's habitual problems. If we're praying for wisdom, those negative patterns can become opportunities to practice new strategies and move our children a little bit in the right direction. As prayer prepares us for the challenges we face with our kids, our anger decreases because we expect God to provide opportunities and we're better prepared to meet them.

One mom said, "I came home from a women's retreat at my church with a renewed commitment to pray for my son. Over the past three weeks, I've seen changes in me and improvement in my relationship with him. I think somehow he can sense that I'm trying to be a better parent, and he's responding with extra effort as well."

God uses his Word to change hearts. "The Word of God is living and active. Sharper than any double-edged sword, it penetrates even to dividing soul and spirit, joints and marrow; it judges the thoughts and attitudes of the heart" (Heb. 4:12). Carefully use God's Word each day to help your kids glimpse a new way of living. The Bible has an amazing way of molding the hearts of our kids.

Use a Systematic Approach to Character Training

When we read passages such as Galatians 5:22–23 and examine the fruit of the Spirit, we see that many of them are character qualities that the Holy Spirit wants to develop in our lives. Patience, joy, love, gentleness, and self-control are some of these.

But how can you, as a parent, help your children to develop character? As family coaches, we (Joanne and Scott) meet with discouraged parents each week. Many of them experience tough child-related problems that require a God-centered character-development plan. You can't create this type of plan in the heat of a discipline problem. Rather, this plan requires you to step back, identify each child's strengths and weaknesses, and devise a systematic approach to changing difficult patterns by moving each child toward developing positive character qualities. You can help your children to make lifestyle changes, develop good habits, and build depth of character. Negative patterns in your children are often a result of a root cause or character-quality deficiency.

As you begin to address character issues in your children, it's helpful to approach them from the perspective of a "parenting doctor." Just as doctors follow specific plans when addressing problems, you can follow a similar six-step plan to identify, analyze, and strategize for positive behavioral change and character development in each child. The six steps are as follows:

1. Observation
2. Diagnosis
3. Solutions
4. Treatment
5. Motivation
6. Follow-up

Step 1: Observation—Recognize the Problem

Begin this process by taking time to identify and write out negative behaviors that need to change. Such behaviors are symptoms of character weaknesses.

To get started, ask yourself questions such as "What is actually happening here?" "What words are being used?" "What don't I like about this?" Many times negative behaviors may seem to be totally independent and unrelated to each other, but as you write them down, you will see patterns of behavior. Don't try to make conclusions; just list as many facts as you can. You won't show this list to each child. It's merely a helpful worksheet for you. Your list may start out like this:

- ☐ didn't finish homework again yesterday
- ☐ leaves room messy
- ☐ doesn't complete chores without being reminded
- ☐ quits a game when not winning
- ☐ hits his brother
- ☐ says, "I can't do it," instead of trying to read difficult words

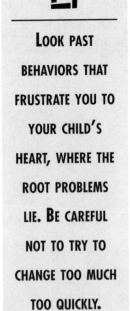

LOOK PAST BEHAVIORS THAT FRUSTRATE YOU TO YOUR CHILD'S HEART, WHERE THE ROOT PROBLEMS LIE. BE CAREFUL NOT TO TRY TO CHANGE TOO MUCH TOO QUICKLY.

(We'll stop here for the sake of illustration, but your list may be several pages long for each child.)

Step 2: Diagnosis—Name the Character Weakness

Once you have your list of negative behaviors, look for patterns. Your list of negative behaviors can be summarized by three or four character weaknesses. In the previous illustration, for example, several problems listed suggest a lack of perseverance or lack of diligence. Look for misbehaviors that are related. Ask yourself questions such as "Do the problems reveal a pattern that happens at a particular time?" "Do the problems occur with certain people?" "Is there an underlying connection that several misbehaviors have in common?"

Try to determine root problems that cause the negative behaviors. Look for character-quality deficiencies. Look past behaviors that frustrate you to each child's heart, where the root problems lie.

Sometimes, as you evaluate the problem behaviors, it's helpful to define negative traits as positive qualities being misused. Good character qualities can be taken to an extreme and demonstrate a negative side. For instance, the organized child may become intolerant or inflexible in a less-structured situation. A child's strength can lead to an area of weakness.

Here's a list of positive character qualities with their negative counterparts. When you see a strength on one side of the list, you're likely to see one or more of the negative expressions of that quality as well.

Positive Quality	Negative Counterpart
Affectionate	Flirtatious, clingy, naive in boy-girl relationships
Analytical	Picky, petty, critical
Compassionate	Easily angered, overly emotional, gullible, biased, lenient
Confident	Prideful, bossy, insensitive, always has to lead, overconfident
Content	Unmotivated, apathetic, lazy
Courageous	Reckless, foolish, can't see consequences of actions
Creative	Deceptive, manipulative, mischievous, always has a better way
Decisive	Inflexible, domineering, impatient
Determined	Hardheaded, stubborn, obstinate, argues, badgers
Discerning	Judgmental, critical, faultfinding, jumps to conclusions

Disciplined	Rigid, bossy, intolerant of change, inflexible, demanding
Eager to please	Compromising, easily tempted, can't take a stand for right
Efficient	Slow, inflexible, demanding, must have things a certain way
Enthusiastic	Intense, insensitive, fanatical, extreme, thrill seeker
Expressive	Talkative, wordy, dominates conversation, poor listener
Flexible	Messy, disorganized, indecisive
Forgiving	Lenient, unable to take a stand for right, people pleaser
Frank	Lacks tact, unloving, not compassionate, insulting, insensitive
Friendly	People pleaser, compromising, avoids being alone
Frugal	Stingy, selfish, judgmental
Generous	Wasteful, gullible, lavish
Grateful	Manipulative, flatterer
Honest	Blunt, brutal, shares too much, insensitive
Hospitable	Cliquish, butters people up
Humble	Self-effacing, shy, embarrassed, lacks initiative, lacks confidence
Independent	Uncooperative, rebellious, aloof, self-centered
Loyal	Possessive, unable to stand for right, too easily influenced
Neat	Perfectionistic, inflexible, unwilling to share, holds back creativity
Objective	Insensitive, uncaring, lacks enthusiasm, critical
Optimistic	Unrealistic, naive, foolish
Patient	Lenient, unwilling to confront
Persuasive	Manipulative, pushy, demanding
Punctual	Intolerant of lateness, impatient, critical

Resourceful	Proud, manipulative, getting around limits
Sensitive	Touchy, easily offended, moody
Thorough	Meticulous, indecisive, hesitant

My (Joanne) son David is sensitive, compassionate, and caring, so he tends to feel things deeply. When he was young, he cried when he saw an ambulance speeding down the road because it meant someone inside was hurt. Unfortunately, sometimes this sensitivity caused him to become moody or overly emotional, pouting or crying over little problems.

My son Timothy, on the other hand, has always had the ability to work hard at a task without being distracted. He can focus intently with real determination to succeed. This quality of persistence can be an asset, but sometimes it shows itself as stubbornness.

Step 3: Solution—Name and Define Each Solution

During the solution step, you determine the character qualities on which each child needs to work. Focus on the positive. One mom, thrilled to discover this step, said, "This is changing the way I relate to my son, Devin. I used to focus on the negative: 'Get your shoes. Clean up your room. Where's your backpack? You left your bike out again.' Now I still have to discipline him, but I've used the character quality of organization to direct my discussion. I feel like I'm teaching him something for the future, not just complaining about the present."

Sometimes a number of character qualities would help your child in a particular area, but start with just one. Be careful not to try to change too much too quickly. (Some children can handle two character-development programs at the same time, but few can handle more than that without feeling overwhelmed.) Choose a name for the quality you want to work on, and then define it in a way that is easy for the child to understand. Don't use dictionary definitions; use working definitions. The name of this positive character

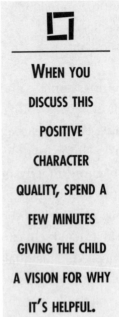

WHEN YOU DISCUSS THIS POSITIVE CHARACTER QUALITY, SPEND A FEW MINUTES GIVING THE CHILD A VISION FOR WHY IT'S HELPFUL.

quality and its definition will provide direction for your child and for you, so it's clear to you both what your child is working on.

Identifying a positive character quality gives each child something to work toward. Many children know their weaknesses all too well. They have become magnets for correction, and they know they disappoint themselves and others with their mistakes. Romans 5:4 says that building character produces hope, an important quality that each child desperately needs.

When you discuss this positive character quality, spend a few minutes giving the child a vision for why it's helpful. You might say, for example, "When you develop this quality in your life, you'll be more successful because ..." A positive character quality gives your child a target to shoot for. Give him or her a vision for change by explaining the value of the particular character quality you'll be working on.

Sometimes people ask us (Scott and Joanne) for our working definitions of certain positive character qualities. Following are some definitions to get you thinking. They will also help you learn how to create your own working definitions. Each one was created to address a specific problem in a family's life. Don't hesitate to change a definition to make it specific to your child. Feel free to use these or modify them based on your children's needs.

☐ Patience: waiting with a happy heart.
☐ Patience: giving others a little more time than I feel comfortable with.

- ☐ Humility: giving God and others credit for their work in my life.
- ☐ Humility: listening to others and rejoicing in their stories instead of having to tell my own.
- ☐ Flexibility: responding with a smile when others interrupt me.
- ☐ Flexibility: changing my plans to help others.
- ☐ Courage: taking a stand for what I know is right.
- ☐ Courage: doing something difficult even though it makes me feel uncomfortable.
- ☐ Resourcefulness: looking for ways to solve my own problems instead of bringing them to others.
- ☐ Resourcefulness: helping others to find solutions when they're stuck.

When my (Scott) son Josh was twelve, Carrie and I wanted to prepare him for the teen years by identifying nine character qualities that contribute to successful adolescence. We created what we call the "Teenage Challenge." We gave him a notebook listing those nine character qualities. We defined each quality in a way that he could understand, included a verse related to each quality for him to memorize, and gave him an activity or assignment to allow him to practice each one. The goal wasn't to develop those qualities in the weeks prior to his birthday, but to identify them for him so he could spend the next several years working on them.

Remember, you're not just dealing with behavioral changes; you're building character. Words such as "stop complaining" focus on behavior. "Gratefulness," on the other hand, is a character quality. A child who is having a hard time staying in bed after saying good night may need to work on self-discipline. Each solution simply identifies and defines the positive quality that will cause the negative behavior(s) to diminish.

Children often like the character-development plan because it gives them a positive way to work on problems they realize they have. Some children may resist the process, but after they see growth, they are often encouraged.

Putting on the pressure is part of the difficult job of parenting. Let's look again at Romans 5:3–4: "Suffering produces perseverance; perseverance, character; and character, hope." You're building character for the long term.

Notice the progression. As you put the pressure on, your children develop perseverance that produces the character that results in hope. This process is not easy most of the time, but it works. We've watched hundreds of parents apply pressure in the right way to their children and see lasting results. Not only are the parents less frustrated, but the kids feel better about themselves, too. It's worth the work.

Step 4: Treatment—Provide Instructions for Working on the Solution

Once you've determined the first positive character quality you want your child to develop, go back to your list of negative behaviors and identify ones that relate. Quite likely, you'll have more than one group of negative behaviors to address.

With your list of negative symptoms on one side of the paper, create a new list identifying how the positive character quality would demonstrate itself. Which specific, positive behaviors could help to define the character quality and replace the negative actions? Be as specific, clear, simple, and practical as possible. This list will become your measuring stick for improvement. Remember, young children are concrete thinkers, so it's important for you to paint the picture of what this new character quality will look like on a day-to-day basis.

For example, your daughter may respond poorly when you give her instructions. She may grumble, complain, or become angry when you ask her to do a task. As you work through the character-development plan, you may determine that she needs the character quality of respectfulness or graciousness. The treatment step asks the question "What would you like your child to do differently?" You might teach her that when you instruct her, she needs to answer, "Okay," and maintain a good attitude.

One dad said, "This step was interesting for us. Sometimes I would get stuck not knowing what a better response would be. When Ryan (age thirteen) was mean to Ricky (age eleven), Ricky became angry, mean, and resentful. But what was a better response? It's hard to experience mistreatment without retaliating. The treatment step gave Ricky and me some great opportunities to talk. I could empathize with him, and he felt like I understood his predicament."

DEVELOPING NEW CHARACTER QUALITIES INVOLVES BREAKING OLD HABITS.

The dad continued. "I saw that I needed to get involved more in their conflict, and I invited Ricky to come to me when he was feeling abused by his brother. I helped him know how to respond with graciousness and forgiveness instead of anger and bitterness. My involvement in the boys' conflict was the single most effective approach I used to connect with Ricky on a deeper level. He grew quite a bit through that."

Of course, it's also important to work with the offender, not just the victim. When children are young, they sometimes hit, kick, bite, or grab when they're trying to solve problems. You may tell them that they need to be kind to each other, but it's best to also give them specific things they can do to demonstrate kindness. Encourage them to talk about the problem, to "use words." When children are very young, tell them exactly which words to use, such as "I don't like it when you do that!" Then teach them that if words don't work effectively, they should get help from a responsible adult, rather than resorting to fighting.

BE POSITIVE WITH YOUR KIDS BY EMPHASIZING SOLUTIONS INSTEAD OF PROBLEMS.

The Turanskys and Millers attended Sandy Cove Bible Conference in Maryland one year where Scott and I (Joanne) spoke. Soon after we arrived, David and Timothy began running down the halls and acting wild. I realized they needed guidance about how to behave in this formal environment. I wanted them to learn how to be respectful and loving to others at the conference center. So I sat down with them and explained that, from now on, we were going to "walk politely" down the halls. Then I explained to them exactly what I meant. I told them they needed to walk slowly and quietly next to me. This rule gave them specific, practical instructions about how to act respectfully in that situation. The boys, in turn, gained a clear understanding of what the new character quality looked like.

Step 5: Motivation—Inspire Change

Determining the right behavior is not enough. The ultimate goal is to help each child want to make right choices. Developing new character qualities involves breaking old habits. Everyone can empathize with a child who is trying to break a habit; it's not easy. When developing positive character qualities in your children, it's important to have a motivational system to help them change and succeed.

Be positive with your kids by emphasizing solutions instead of problems. In fact, receiving a parent's praise may be all the motivation that's necessary to change a particular problem once a child recognizes it and knows what to do instead. People (children and adults) feel good about themselves when they do the right things. That internal motivation is powerful. Encourage it whenever possible.

People occasionally ask, "Why should we reward children for doing something they should be doing already, such as cleaning their rooms?" That's a good question and can be answered when we understand the difference between internal and external motivation.

Internal or intrinsic motivation is that inner drive to do what's right, the desire to make wise choices. We want to develop internal motivation in our children. External motivation sometimes becomes the vehicle to do just that.

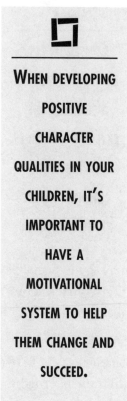

WHEN DEVELOPING POSITIVE CHARACTER QUALITIES IN YOUR CHILDREN, IT'S IMPORTANT TO HAVE A MOTIVATIONAL SYSTEM TO HELP THEM CHANGE AND SUCCEED.

External or extrinsic motivation comes from outside a person. Consequences, both positive and negative, are external attempts to motivate children in the right direction. We typically view these as behavior-modification techniques. A parent might say, for example, "You can watch a video after you get your homework done," or "Clean up your room, and then you can go out and play." Behavior modification works in the short run because it allows children to have something they want if they'll do what their parents say. Unfortunately, in the long run these children often don't develop character. They learn to do good things when there is something in it for them.

The key to using external motivation appropriately is to tie character into your plan. Then you're working more deeply to shape your child's heart. The principle to remember is that *external motivation is helpful if it builds internal motivation.* If you give an external reward when your child completes a task, talk about the internal quality you're wanting your child to develop and why it's beneficial. You might say something like, "You are developing thoroughness by putting those clothes away. You may go out and play now."

When I (Scott) was a child, I had a "star chart" for memorizing Bible verses. Some people could argue that I was more interested in getting a star than I was about learning verses, but my parents used an external system to give me a love and appreciation for memorizing God's Word. I still memorize Scripture today. Just as it did with me, external motivation can help build positive or negative associations with specific behaviors and give your children an internal desire to do the right thing.

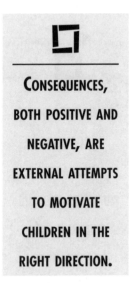

CONSEQUENCES, BOTH POSITIVE AND NEGATIVE, ARE EXTERNAL ATTEMPTS TO MOTIVATE CHILDREN IN THE RIGHT DIRECTION.

Take advantage of opportunities to affirm internal motivation in your children. When Jill puts her toys back on the shelf after playing with them, you may say to her, "I'll bet you feel pretty good when you clean up after yourself, don't you?" This reinforces her positive feelings of accomplishment and independence.

Step 6: Follow-up—Continue to Work on Solutions

Character is built over time. Don't expect huge changes in your children overnight. Many little steps are more realistic and effective in bringing about lasting changes than large steps. Therefore, reinforce "approximately" right behavior whenever you can. Don't wait for absolutely right behavior before offering encouragement.

Continue to concentrate on one particular character quality for a period of time in order to bring about the desired results in each child. As he or she makes progress, continue to talk about the importance of this character quality. Gently offer reminders when negative patterns reappear.

Three Factors to Remember

You may feel that progress is slow and end up asking yourself, *Am I getting anywhere?* If you feel discouraged, consider three things.

First, keep in mind that you're building a tape in your child's head. To understand the idea of building a tape, think about some things your parents taught you: "Turn off the lights before you leave the room"; "Eat your vegetables"; "Be nice to your sister"; "Say excuse me." Did you heed their instructions? Maybe not as much as your parents would have liked, yet their words still play back in your head. Parents don't always see the impact of their words. But your kids are listening, and you're building a tape in their heads as you lovingly and consistently prod them to action.

Second, pray for your children often. Pray that God will use your words and actions to make lasting, positive changes in their lives. God is at work for the long term. He is in the process of changing people and molding hearts that follow after him.

Third, if you find that you're encountering a lot of resistance from your child, consider his or her relationships and activities. Sometimes a child's environment works against the very character you're trying to develop. Bad influences can be a challenging enemy. First Corinthians 15:33 reads, "Bad company corrupts good character." Bad influences in your child's life, such as negative friendships, are at the top of the list. Limit them (or eliminate them altogether if possible), but don't just target people as the only bad influences in your child's life. Reading material and entertainment choices also affect children and youth.

One mom said, "I realized that my daughter was getting her ideas for books to read from a popular teen magazine. I helped her see that there were other books that had better values, and I showed her how to locate them. I helped her find more appropriate reading material that fit better for developing her character."

It's Worth It!

In the end, a character-development approach to child training pays huge dividends. Children may forget the individual issues, but they will remember the character qualities. You can successfully address deep-rooted problems in children's lives over time through a character-based approach.

Here's a quick summary of the six-step plan for character development.

1. Observation: recognize the problem.
2. Diagnosis: name the character weakness.
3. Solution: name and define each solution.
4. Treatment: provide instructions for working on the solution.
5. Motivation: inspire change.
6. Follow-up: continue to work on solutions.

Appendix

Break vs. Time Out

Many Christians have a hard time with Time Out, and for good reasons. Typically *Time Out* is a term used for isolating a child for a set period of time as a punishment for doing wrong, and it can be counterproductive to the discipline process. Expecting children to solve problems alone is unrealistic. Furthermore, the isolation can appear to force children away from the parent's love.

A Break is a more valuable technique because it focuses on the heart and teaches children a more accurate picture of reality. When a child takes a Break, the separation means missing out. The child is then motivated to repent in order to return to the benefits of family life. Using Breaks enables us to discipline our kids with the principle of separation, in much the same way God does with his children. Instead of punishment by isolation, the Bible teaches discipline by separation.

When we enter God's family, we receive forgiveness through Christ, but when we sin, we are spiritually separated from fellowship with him. God hates sin, so when we disobey him, we experience separation as a natural consequence of disobedience. We experience this separation through guilt and a lack of peace and thus are motivated to repent and regain intimate fellowship with God. This is how God uses separation from fellowship to motivate us to repentance. However, because he is spirit, God never physically separates himself from us, and he lovingly waits for us to return to him with confession and repentance.

There are two factors that draw our children back to us in repentance. First, in 1 Corinthians 5:2, Paul expressed that there should be grief or sorrow over sin. Likewise, when parents reflect sadness instead of anger, they provide an effective motivation for their children to change their hearts. The disappointment seen in a parent's eyes can be a powerful incentive for a child to want to change. Therefore, when you send your child to take a Break, be careful about your anger. It just gets in the way of what God wants to do. Reflect sorrow instead.

A second motivation to return to the parent is the fact that the child is missing out on activities and other privileges. You'll need to suspend the child's benefits of family life while he or she is working on the heart. Children learn that they cannot enjoy the benefits of family life without abiding by the principles that make it work.

Let's say that four-year-old Susan becomes angry at the park and pushes her friend. Mom says, "Susan, that's not kind. You need to sit here under the tree and take a Break." Because Susan has experienced Breaks many times before, she knows what to do. She sits under the tree for a few minutes, then comes back to Mom to discuss the problem. Her motivation to talk to Mom is fueled by the fact that she is missing out on park time.

In the New Testament, when a believer was unresponsive to correction, the consequence was separation from the benefits of church fellowship. In Matthew 18, Jesus established a pattern for discipline within the church that had, as its final consequence, separation or excommunication. In 1 Corinthians 5, Paul encouraged the church to put an unrepentant man out of the body. This separation would cause the offender to miss the benefits of fellowship and motivate repentance. Because separation can motivate repentance, a Break is a helpful part of the discipline process, not just simply a consequence.

During a Time Out, a child serves a sentence for a crime committed. The parent's role is that of a police officer, to keep that child in Time Out until the sentence is served. During a Break, the parent's role is similar to that of the prodigal son's father, who waited with open arms for the child to return. How refreshing that is for us whose children require a lot of discipline. The concept of a Break shifts the responsibility from parental control to the child's repentance. That truth alone makes a Break the better approach.

READERS' GUIDE

*For Personal Reflection or
Group Discussion*

READERS' GUIDE

I found one!" Timothy exclaimed as he looked under the pillow.
"I've got one, too!" David joined in as he reached to the top of
the piano.

Anticipation filled the air as my (Joanne) boys searched the living room.

Little chocolate eggs were hiding on window sills, behind pillows, and under tables. They were nestled in planters and the arms of chairs. David and Timothy ran from one corner of the room to the other and then into the hallway, searching as they went.

The flurry of enthusiasm continued for several minutes, then quieted. Were all the eggs discovered? Were there places the boys hadn't searched? Each boy glanced down at his stash. What a treasure! Could there be more?

Three days later, one lone chocolate egg sat perched above the closet door.

I saw it every time I walked through the hall, but no one else did. It stayed there ... waiting to be discovered.

This book reveals eight tools to help you become a more effective parent. Others are yet to be discovered.

As you finish reading this book, what is God telling you about your family?

You know the strengths and weaknesses of each family member; so does God.

Think about where your family is and where you are going. The following readers' guide can help you continue to apply what you have been learning.

Answers to your unique problems and situations are available in this book and elsewhere. Look around. Seek help. Ask questions. Before you know it, you'll be adding more tools to your toolbox and developing the resources you need to do the best kind of home improvement—the kind that will last forever.

CHAPTER 1

1. Why do we teach children obedience?

2. Read 1 Samuel 15:22. According to this verse, what does God think about obedience?

3. Describe some examples from the Bible where God demonstrated a tight Action Point.

4. What are the advantages and disadvantages of using anger to motivate your Action Point?

5. What are some cues that indicate you are about to get to your Action Point, and how long does it take for you to reach it?

6. How can we balance a tight Action Point with the biblical concept of grace as we discipline our children?

CHAPTER 2

1. The Positive Conclusion helps people think rightly about mistakes. What are some of the ways children think wrongly about mistakes? How might some adults think wrongly about mistakes that they've made?

2. After the sin of David and Bathsheba was exposed, the consequence was that the baby died. Shortly afterward, the couple got pregnant again. God told David to name the baby Jedidiah, which means "loved by the LORD." How was God's response through the prophet like a Positive Conclusion to David? (See 2 Sam. 12:24–25.)

3. In Jesus' interaction with Peter after the resurrection, he sought to reaffirm Peter and have a Positive Conclusion. After all, the last time Jesus saw Peter was when Peter denied him three times. How was Jesus' response in John 21:15–19 like the ending statement, "Go ahead and try again"?

4. The Positive Conclusion is a structure for processing offenses. Some children will go through the motions without the right

heart attitude. How might you respond to a child who doesn't seem to be changing on a deeper level and just wants to get through the process?

CHAPTER 3

1. According to Matthew 15:19 and Proverbs 4:23, why is the heart so important?

2. Using the chart in this chapter, identify some of the benefits of the Break approach verses the Time Out approach to correction.

3. Think of a time in your life when you made a significant heart change. What was the change, and what kinds of things motivated that change in your life?

4. What are some examples of heart issues you wish would change in your son or daughter?

5. What are some ways that you might challenge your child on a heart level to make significant changes?

6. Why is prayer helpful when raising children?

CHAPTER 4

1. Identify the values behind these common rules in family life.

   ✖ Come straight home after school.

   ✖ Be off the phone by 9:00 p.m.

   ✖ Don't hit your brother.

   ✖ Say excuse me before interrupting.

   ✖ Clean up after yourself.

2. Identify rules that will teach the following values:

- ❁ Self-discipline

- ❁ Responsibility

- ❁ Respect

- ❁ Thoughtfulness

- ❁ Cooperation

3. Parents teach their children manners so that they will be more successful in relationships. But too much emphasis on manners can ruin a meal or set a critical tone in the family. How do you balance your desire to allow kids to be kids with the need for them to learn to be socially appropriate?

4. Read Matthew 23:23–26. How did the Pharisees get their values and rules mixed up, motivating Jesus to call them hypocrites?

5. What is the danger of emphasizing rules too much in family life? What is the danger of not providing enough rules for children?

CHAPTER 5

1. List some of your children's pet peeves or things that spark anger.

2. What are the early physical signals that indicate you're getting angry? What are the early cues for your child?

3. Children without a plan usually resort to yelling or violence to solve problems. What are some good elements in an anger-management plan for your child?

4. What ways do your children try to draw you into a fight when they are angry? How can you stop yourself from jumping in?

5. What do the following verses teach about anger? How can you apply them to your children?

  ▓ Proverbs 22:24

  ▓ Proverbs 29:11

  ▓ Proverbs 30:33

CHAPTER 6

1. Read 1 Corinthians 13:4–7 and James 1:12 and note the word *persevere*. What can parents learn about perseverance from these verses?

2. Thinking long term (principle 4) means that we anticipate future benefits from the present challenges. How will it help your children later if you teach them now to clean their rooms? Report back after doing a task? Resolve conflict peacefully with a sibling?

3. Bedtimes are often a challenge in families. What do they teach children, and what benefit do they provide for kids both short term and long term?

4. Name a few of the key things you wish you could teach your children before they are launched into adulthood. Take one and describe ways you are, or could be, teaching it now.

5. Identify a difference in parenting philosophy between you and your spouse or another parent. What underlying values contribute to each philosophy? (For example: one parent is strict and another is lenient.) What are the advantages of each?

CHAPTER 7

1. Describe one valuable lesson you learned from experience (driving, shopping, listening to sales presentations, etc.).

2. In the following Bible stories, which technique was used: open-ended questions, natural consequences, or logical consequences?

   ❈ Genesis 4:5–7

   ❈ Genesis 12:10–20

   ❈ Jonah 4

3. Jesus promised the Holy Spirit to his disciples in John 16:7–14. How does the Holy Spirit exemplify the counselor or coach role in our lives as God's children (i.e., encouragement, correction, guidance)? How can you take advantage of the Holy Spirit's role in your children's lives?

4. Solving your own problem builds confidence. How can you help children develop self-confidence while at the same time teach them to trust in the Lord for his solutions to their problems?

CHAPTER 8

1. What is one character quality you'd like to see your child develop, and how might you define it in positive terms to address your specific situation?

2. What are some of the internal and external motivations that God uses in our lives to guide us?

3. Galatians 5:22–23 lists several character qualities. According to this passage, how are they obtained? How does this affect the way you help your children change?

4. As you look at the list of character qualities misused, identify one that you would like to work on for yourself and explain why.